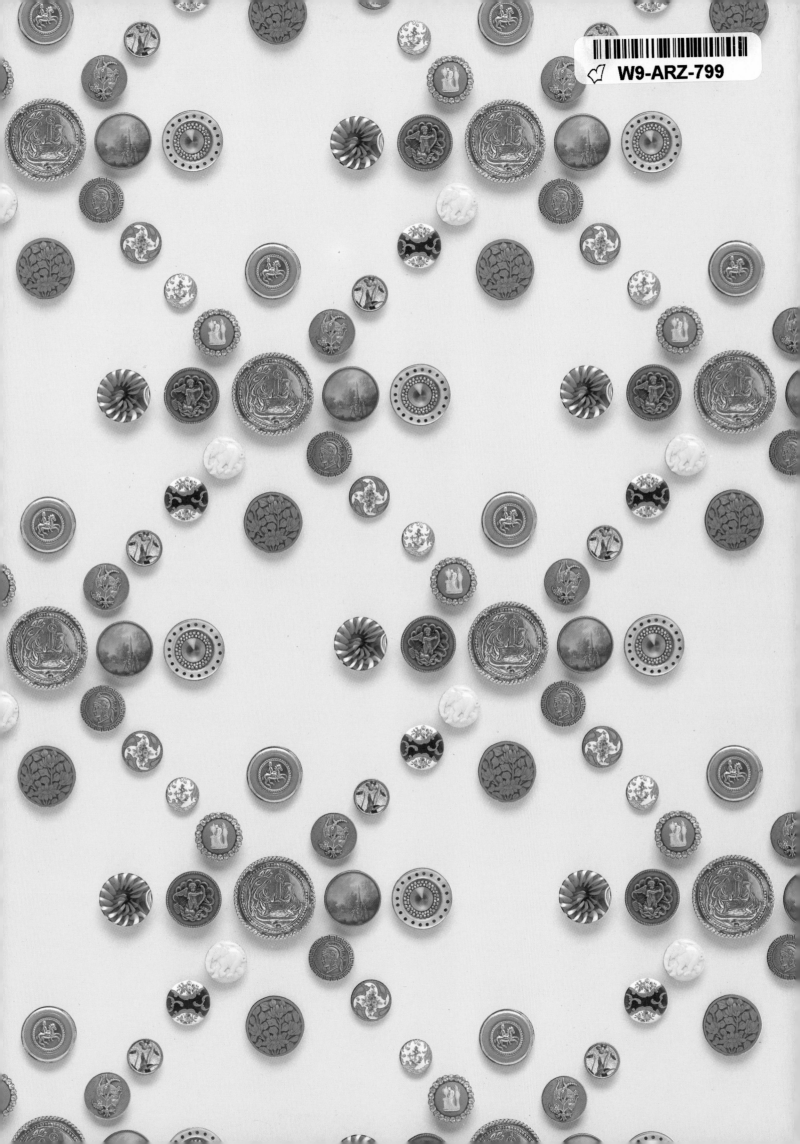

BUTTONS

BUTTONS

THE COLLECTOR'S GUIDE TO SELECTING, RESTORING, AND ENJOYING NEW AND VINTAGE BUTTONS

Nancy Fink and Maryalice Ditzler

COURAGE BOOKS

AN IMPRINT OF
RUNNING PRESS
PHILADELPHIA, PENNSYLVANIA

Canadian Representatives:
General Publishing Co., Ltd.
30 Lesmill Road, Don Mills
Ontario M3B 2T6

9 8 7 6 5 4 3 2 1
Digit on the right indicates the number of this printing

Library of Congress
Cataloging-in-Publication Number
92-54940

ISBN 1-56138-215-9

This book was designed and produced by
Quintet Publishing Limited
6 Blundell Street
London N7 9BH

Creative Director: Richard Dewing
Project Editor: Stefanie Foster
Designer: Nicky Chapman
Editor: Maggi McCormick
Photographer: Harry Rinker Jnr.

Typeset in Great Britain by
Central Southern Typesetters, Eastbourne
Manufactured in Singapore by
Bright Arts Pte Limited
Printed in Hong Kong by
Leefung-Asco Printers Limited

First published by Courage Books
an imprint of Running Press Book Publishers
125 South Twenty-second Street
Philadelphia, Pennsylvania 19103–4399

C O N T E N T S

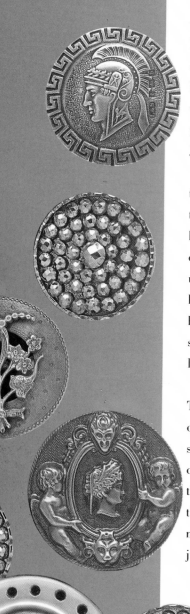

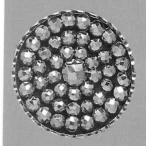

·········· INTRODUCTION ··········

Button collecting is an organized hobby which has infected thousands of people over the years as a way to study art, history, sociology, economics, and politics. How could the collecting of such a small practical item cause anyone to become engrossed in such deep study? The buttons reflect when and how they were manufactured. They show what people valued in an era and what the fashion of the time was. Judgments can be made based on the buttons people wore.

What is a *button?* Collectors define a button as something that could be sewn to a garment either by some type of shank or through holes drilled in the button. The purpose of these buttons is to act as a fastener, although some were used only as ornamentation. Thus, buttons are associated with costume and uniform. Many collectors, however, also search for related-button items like buttonhooks, studs and cuff buttons, bridle buttons, and shoe button covers. Buttons, although small in size, can become invasive unless the collector is selective, learning which buttons to buy and which to pass by.

Buttons should be carefully chosen rather than amassed. Therefore, a collector does not speak of how many buttons he or she owns, but about how each button or group of buttons shows some unique characteristic of a medium or the classification. But, buttons are fun and whimsical. They show the artistry and the humor of their makers and wearers. Look at the faces painted on bone underwear buttons, as well as the magnificent plique-à-jour enamel ones. And, some buttons are just plain ugly.

So begin your search for the buttons you like as we did a few years ago. Let the operative words be "the ones you like," since it is hard to keep collecting something just for its value. Your favorite button may have value only to you. Let your collecting lead to study of the button and its time. Then, your mind grows along with your collection. Make the hobby one in which you can relax from the stresses of the modern world. Better yet, join a club so that you can learn from experienced collectors who will help you determine the best buttons to buy and those to avoid. The National Button Society and the British Button Society are two organizations with worldwide membership and periodicals to assist collectors. Their addresses are listed at the back of this book.

As a collector, you also have the obligation of preserving and presenting the buttons in a manner that ensures their survival. Avoid storage of materials which will interact chemically, thus causing deterioration. Buttons are often scratched when they are stored in jars or boxes, so mounting on acid-free boards helps protect them. Learn the best ways in which to clean your buttons so that the beauty of each comes through as you show off your collection. With a collection also comes the responsibility of curating.

The buttons shown in this book are ones we have collected, and most are available from button dealers today. These are not the most spectacular buttons available, but ones that most collectors can find, although some are rare and finding them will cause you to hunt.

An Historical Overview

CHAPTER I

Looking at the small plain buttons which are used on men's, women's, and children's clothing today, people might wonder why someone would be interested in collecting buttons. These utilitarian items are fasteners with only a functional value, following the axiom of the modern world, "Form follows function." This simplicity is what modern clothing demands since the color or weave of the fabric or the style of the garment is often the distinctive feature. For most people, the plain-styled – classic – garment with matching plain classic buttons is what is desirable. In the past, however, fashion dictated other styles, and the button industry responded with buttons that were works of art – often the jewelry of the day. Even the smallest button created interest. This art in miniature is one thing that draws today's collectors into the enchantment of the world of buttons.

·········· THE EARLIEST BUTTONS ··········

Probably serving as ornaments, seals, and badges rather than fasteners, the earliest buttons were hand-wrought by smiths or carvers. Prehistoric man is credited with inventing buttons and toggles. The Greeks and Romans used large buttons to gather fabric in tunics and gowns, and the barbaric, nomadic tribes that swept out of the Asian steppes fastened their cloaks and capes with button-like closures. The button collector is unlikely to find such items since these artifacts are of museum quality, but the concept of buttons following the dictates of fashion is well-established even in this early history.

With the fall of Rome in 476 AD and the coming of the Dark Ages, fashion history records that men and women wore very similar clothing – loose-fitting, shift-like garments with the length often determined by the social rank of the wearer. The higher the rank, usually, the longer the garment. Buttons were rarely part of this attire. The knight of the medieval period might have used a button to close his cloak or to fasten his garments under his armor, and as clothing became more fitted in the twelfth and thirteenth centuries, buttons became important. In fact, the Crusaders, who are credited with bringing so many things (including the rose) from their battles in the Middle East, are believed to have introduced the buttonhole to Europe. This significant invention had a great impact on fashion, since fabric could now be overlapped and buttoned; previously fabric had to be butted, and a toggle was looped over the button to close the garment.

.... THE RENAISSANCE ....

The use of buttons increased with the Renaissance when fashion dictated that men wear doublets, fitted jackets with narrowing, almost leg-of-mutton, sleeves. Close-fitting doublets were tightly secured from chin to waist and from elbow to knuckle by rows and rows of buttons. Breeches were fastened at the thigh or knee, as well as the waist, with buttons which also served as ornamentation and decoration. Women, however, were usually laced into their gowns, so the use of buttons on female clothing was simply decorative, and the importance of buttons for men's clothing dominated the industry until the mid-nineteenth century. Thus, the glitter and gleam of the gold and silver, enhanced by semi-precious and precious stones, was part of a man's world of fashion.

Wood, bone, brass, and pewter were used in button creations which became part of the costume of the common man; while the wealthy, including the growing middle class as well as the nobility, had artists and artisans fashion their treasures. Button guilds had been established in Paris in the thirteenth century and worked only in the specific materials with which they had been trained. Some countries enacted laws to restrict the use of certain materials in buttons, thus, the use of the silver button, particularly combined with the toggle so that the button could be removed and worn with another suit of clothes, became fashionable. The earliest buttons that collectors find today are seventeenth century Dutch silver ones; unfortunately, the toggle has often been removed, since, it would seem, the button with only a shank would be more valuable to some collectors than one with an attached toggle.

BELOW
Dutch silver buttons of the late seventeenth century were often large, with toggles that have since become detached. Hand stamping or jewels and enameling created the design. All were worn on heavy linen or woolen jackets or cloaks.
1. Square stamped in conventional design. A heavy shank with toggle taken off; *c.* 1700.
2. Open-work silver button with heavy shank. The toggle is lost. 1 in/2.5 cm high with gemstones laid into the design.
3. Button with 1½ in/4 cm toggle showing. Stamped design.

·········· THE GOLDEN AGE ··········

The eighteenth century is the golden age for buttons, and collectors thirst after examples, since the workmanship and artistry mirror the finest creations of the period, particularly in France and England. Louis XIV and his court set the standard. Men wore long vests and matching overcoats with wide lapels. Sets of buttons adorned the closure of the vest and the lapels. Smaller matching sleeve or cuff buttons fastened the tight-fitting arm of the garment and were repeated on the tightly closed knee of the breeches. Louis wore buttons highly decorated with precious metals and stones; diamonds, along with other stones, and gold were used in the early eighteenth century. Fabric buttons made of the same cloth as the garment were highly decorated with lace and embroidery of the most intricate detail. Gold and silver floss were combined with the finest lace and silk. Competition over the ownership of the finest sets of buttons meant that rivals hired the best artists, like Watteau and Boucher, to create them. In fact, all the countries in Europe had extremely busy button trades by the eighteenth century.

In England the button industry flourished. Experimentation with new materials led to the famous steel designs of Matthew Boulton and the ceramic jasperware of Josiah Wedgwood. In fact, some of the most desirable buttons are the eighteenth-century combination of a jasperware plaque in a Boulton steel frame. Further, the development in France of the "under-glass" frame, in which the design was mounted under a piece of glass with a metal back secured to the other

BELOW

Decorated pearl buttons in sets of 20–24 enhanced the coats of the courtiers and showed off the skills of button makers in the eighteenth century.

1. Decorated with steel cups and cut steel heads; a jewel simulating a diamond has been added to the center; carved edges to enhance the design. Worn in sets on men's coats in the late 1700s.
2. A coaching scene on a 2 in/5 cm disk which is incised and painted with black ink to show up the design. A set may have shown various scenes or been uniform; c 1800.

LEFT

The eighteenth century was the height of button fashion for men's clothes, and the artistry and craftsmanship of the button makers was obvious.

1.,2. Small jewel-like breeches buttons with foil reflecting through the heavy glass mounted in a silver back; used at the knee of the breeches, c 1770.
3. Reverse painting on glass protected by copper collet; worn in sets on men's coats in the late 1700s.
4. Habitat button with small animals and plants inside protected under glass with copper collet; worn in sets on men's coats, c 1770s.
5. The first under-glass designs were foils painted to match the fabric; worn in sets of 20–24 on men's coats.

parts by a copper collet, allowed artists to incorporate materials and designs impossible before. Ivory could be intricately carved and mounted over foil; small miniature paintings on ivory, silk, or paper could be painted in a variety of media; reverse painting could be executed on the back of the glass; even small plants and animals could be put in the frame to form "habitat" buttons. The development of the porcelain of Meissan, Limoges, and Staffordshire meant that sets of buttons were available for costumes. Style demanded elegance, and button manufacturers responded.

The wealthy set the fashion, the masses imitated, and the button developed its second concept. First, buttons follow fashion; then, buttons are created to imitate the original artistry. The use of glass and enameling was developed to imitate the use of semi-precious and precious stones. Pastes, or *strass*, were set to imitate diamonds. Steel buttons imitated silver, and pinchbeck, an alloy of copper and zinc which imitated gold, became commonplace. Other metals, like brass and pewter, could be stamped to look hand-chased.

···· THE INDUSTRIAL REVOLUTION ····

The Industrial Revolution of the late eighteenth and nineteenth century greatly advanced the button industry. The die-maker carefully cut punches and dies so that, as the factory advanced mechanically, thousands of buttons could be produced. The die-makers were so important to the button companies that in Britain their emigration was prohibited for fear that the manufacturing secrets would be taken abroad. That is exactly what happened: plans were smuggled out of England, and companies in Attleboro, Massachusetts, and Waterbury, Connecticut, became the American centers for metal buttons. The War of 1812 provided the impetus for the growth of an industry which still produces uniform buttons in Connecticut today.

Until the mid-nineteenth century, buttons were worn only by men. Even in the United States, the young country founded on democratic rule, men wore intricately designed brass buttons brushed with a gold wash, called "Golden Age," highly prized by collectors. Small vest buttons picturing the American eagle, a sheaf of wheat, the Tom Thumb railroad

BELOW
Called "Golden Age" buttons by collectors, these American-made gilt buttons were used in the 1820s and 1830s in sets of six or eight on men's jackets.

1. Called a watch case for its flat top and sloping sides resembling a man's watch case; 1 in/2.5 cm; c 1830.
2.,5. Conventional, non-pictorial designs, hand chased.
3.,4.,6. Pictorials, hand-chased, typically of plant life with flowers and fruit.

engine, and other symbols of America, called "Jacksonians"
by collectors, were worn only by men. Even small glass
buttons collected on charm-strings by girls prior to their
weddings were men's vest buttons. But, times were changing.
Parisian fashion houses began to use buttons on women's
clothing. They were sometimes made of matching fabric and
had molded tops of various designs, but metal, pearl, clear or
colored glass, and black glass were also added to the materials
used by the early manufacturers. In addition, china companies
like Minton introduced utilitarian china buttons decorated
with transfers or stenciled with colors to match or contrast with
the dress fabric.

The Japanese influence was also felt when in 1854 Matthew
Perry, an American naval officer, negotiated a treaty which
opened the ports of Japan to western trade. Europeans,
particularly the French in the 1860s and 1870s, popularized
the arts of Japan in a movement termed *Japanisme*. Markets in

1   2   3   4   5

England and France were flooded with porcelain buttons with a characteristic crackle glaze stippled with gold made in the Satsuma region of Japan. Lacquerware, both Japanese and Chinese, became extremely popular, and red cinnabar was also imported. Silver, ivory, enamel, and inlays of pearl with oriental motifs became popular and were imitated by western manufacturers. Collectors often find buttons which appear to be of Japanese or Chinese origin, only to find them of western manufacture, influenced by artists like Whistler. These imports from the Far East did not end until the 1960s, so collectors must make a careful study to determine any button's age. In general, the workmanship is finer and the quality higher on the older buttons.

####### THE VICTORIAN INFLUENCE ·······

No other single person since Louis XIV had as much impact on the button industry as Queen Victoria. During her long reign, she set all the social trends, and fashion, including her style and use of buttons, was no exception. The most significant influence was caused by the death of her husband Albert, the Prince Consort, in 1861 and the subsequent mourning period of over 25 years. Overnight the black glass industry, centered in the Gablonz area of today's Czechoslovakia, became highly active, and black remained the predominant fashion color for over two decades. Black glass buttons, meant to imitate the queen's Whitby mourning jet, were produced by the ton. Decorations were few, but designs were plentiful. The buttons were molded in forms made by the same die-making process used for metal buttons; often the same button design can be found in metal, black glass, and clear or colored glass.

ABOVE
Western buttons of the late 1800s displaying Oriental motifs.

1. The sweeping tail of the rooster is reminiscent of Japanese designs; worn as decoration; brass; 1 in/2.5 cm.
2. Pressed wood, self-shank with plain conical back; 1 in/2.5 cm; c 1880.
3. Two different-colored metals reminiscent of Japanese metal work; ¾ in/2 cm.
4. Octagon with Oriental woman with a fan like Mme Butterfly or Mme Chrysanthemum; intricate Oriental border scroll; molded black glass; c 1880.
5. Oriental man painted on steel disk.

BELOW
Queen Victoria's influence on the button-making industry was so great that buttons commemorating her coronation and jubilees, as well as those which reflect her taste, are collected.

1. Molded black glass to imitate fabric; probably made in Bohemia; 1 in/2.5 cm; c 1880–1910.
2.,3.,5.,8. Buttons in metal and celluloid-protected lithograph (8.) to commemorate Victoria's 1887 Jubilee. Worn by supporters on lapels.
4. ½ in/1.3 cm brass buttons, celebrating the young Queen's coronation in 1837.
6. Paisley design reflecting Oriental influence; 1 in/2.5 cm.
7. ¾ in/2 cm button for the 1887 Jubilee; the rose, shamrock, and thistle are symbolic of the unity of the kingdom.

1   2   3   4   5   6   7   8

RIGHT

Picture buttons of the late nineteenth century were created in many materials and can be grouped in themes. Couples are the theme here. All were worn on jackets, dresses, and blouses.

1. Thin sheet of celluloid stamped with press of design, called "The Kiss by the Wall;" 1 in/2.5 cm; c 1880.
2. 1 in/2.5 cm enamel with champlevé border of couple in eighteenth-century costume. Probably made in France around 1870.
3. 1 in/2.5 cm brass button showing scene from Wagner opera; c 1885; often worn by opera fans.
4. Romeo and Juliet in 1¼ in/3 cm brass button with original red finish to match fabric; c 1880.
5. Caramel glass with gold luster added; plate and loop shank; ¾ in/2.5 cm.
6. Priscilla and John Alden brass pieces applied to leather background; 1½ in/3.3 cm with brass frame; c 1880.
7. Ceramic button with black silhouette transfer; painted gold rim.

BELOW

Manufacturers often used the same design in a variety of materials.

1.,2.,3. 1. 2 in/5 cm bear claw in yellow imitation tortoise glass with loop metal shank, and cone shank; 2. brass, 1 in/2.5 cm; 3. black glass, 1½ in/3 cm with plate-and-loop shank; c 1880.
4.,5. Genghis Khan arriving in the village; 2 in/5 cm buttons: molded blue glass in metal frame, celluloid fitted tightly in japanned back with gold and silver paint; c 1890–1910.

Each stage of Queen Victoria's reign is reflected in buttons. When Victoria became Empress of India, button makers used the symbol of the paisley on all materials. For each jubilee commemorative buttons were issued; in fact, the queen's image is so popular with collectors that many set aside part of their collections for Victoria and her line.

The age of Victoria is also the time of the "Picture Button." New plays, operettas, novels, poems, or paintings sent the die-makers to their benches to create new dies. People could show their approval of a new work of art by wearing several buttons derived from it on a shirtwaist, a coat, or a cloak. Women even decorated their skirts with these buttons. Every Wagner opera or Gilbert and Sullivan operetta had a series of buttons depicting various characters or events. Favorite nursery rhymes and the drawings of children's illustrators, like Kate Greenaway, were featured on buttons; often there were several variations of the same story. Some collectors spend years identifying a picture button with the work of literature, art, or music to which it refers. Most collections contain examples of picture buttons from very small to very large size, and these highly prized items often bring high prices based not only on the rarity of the button, but also on the demand collectors put on owning pictorials.

BELOW

BELOW
Modern button makers have created buttons with traditional designs, copying old techniques but using new materials.

1. Copper metal, commemorative of Queen Elizabeth II's coronation in 1952; 2in/5cm.
2. Called the "Flower Seller;" one-piece stamped button; 2 in/5 cm, white metal.
3. Molded plastic of Mary Queen of Scots; 1½ in/3 cm.
4. Design under plexiglass of cutout of couple; similar to eighteenth-century work; mounted in wood frame; 1 in/2.5 cm.

RIGHT
Modern button-makers have used new materials to create designs which have been described as very up-to-date.

1. Plaster of Paris used in 1940s and 1950s because metal was scarce; knitting cat with painted yarn and needles; 2½ in/6 cm long.
2. Molded plastic wood made by Burwood and Syroco; worn by boys in 1930s; part of set with knights and weapons; 1½ in/3.8 cm.
3. Lucite realistic basket with painted flowers; worn in 1940s and 1950s on women's jackets or dresses.
4. Colored plastic rectangle with carved and painted reverse; fishing scene; worn on jackets or dresses; c 1940.

········ The Twentieth Century ········

The Art Nouveau period and the time before World War I saw a growth in the silver industry in England, and collectors seek silver buttons with the hallmarks of the assay office in a British city. In addition, large cloak buttons set with a center piece of glass to imitate a semi-precious stone were worn on women's evening cloaks and formal coats. These "Gay '90s" are sought by collectors for their variety of color and cut of the "stone."

In 1918 the war ended, and with it the period of "old buttons" for the collector. From that point on, collectors talk about modern buttons. Modern manufacturers have introduced many new materials or extended the use of late nineteenth-century industrial materials into the world of buttons. Fashion, however, has dictated more tailored clothing with plainer buttons and often darker colors. The shirt button of the 1920s has become the model for buttons on all garments – dresses, blouses, suits, and shirts. Occasionally, whimsical styles – the transparent glass of the 1940s in all colors; the molded, extruded wood of Syroco or Burwood of the 1920s and 1930s; the colorful Bakelite of the 1940s and 1950s; or the lucite buttons of the 1950s – have been introduced. Colorful glass buttons from West Germany appeared after World War II and were popular; millions were imported into the United States until the early 1960s. But mankind and womankind wanted easy-care buttons which could withstand the washing machine and the dryer: the small, two- or four-hole, flat, plastic button could. Who could have known that it was the descendant of such magnificent buttons as collectors seek?

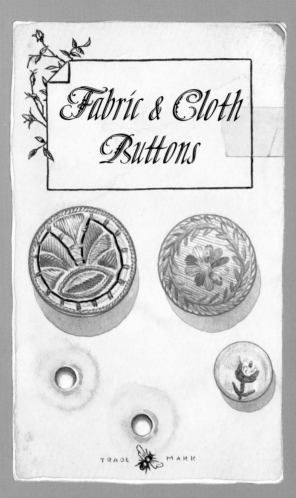

Fabric & Cloth Buttons

TRADE MARK

CHAPTER 2

There have been cloth buttons from the earliest days of button making. Small disks of bone or wood were covered by pieces of cloth which matched or contrasted with the garment. Circles of cloth, drawn together and stitched tightly at the back, could then be decorated on top with lace, embroidery, sets of gems, etc. Collectors have not always valued these fabric buttons, but their workmanship and history make them worthy of consideration.

····· **HANDMADE FABRIC BUTTONS** ·····

In France and England, medieval embroidery guilds were important, and Parisian button guilds established in the thirteenth century included ones which dealt only in decorated fabric buttons. Lace-makers were protected by Louis XIV for their role in the creation of beautiful buttons. In England a law outlawing cloth-covered buttons was passed in 1685 to protect manufacturers of metal buttons, implying that cloth buttons were much in demand. Laws in some countries forbade the use of luxurious materials like gold and semi-precious gems in buttons, but allowed the use of silver and cloth.

The production of cloth buttons was scarcely impeded by the law, and the industry flourished. Highly embroidered, and highly fashionable, buttons on silk, satin, and linen were found in sets to match garments. Gold and silver floss were intertwined with brightly colored silk floss, and the design was only limited by the skill of the embroiderer or the desire of the tailor. These rare eighteenth-century embroideries are sought by collectors; they are scarce because fabric buttons became easily soiled and frayed around the edges. In addition, since the buttons were made to match exactly, the owner of the garment might not have removed them to use on another suit of clothes. Museums may have clothing from the seventeenth and eighteenth century with the cloth buttons still in place, while the metal ones might have been removed. The buttons that had been removed are most accessible to today's collector.

Another highly prized eighteenth-century fabric button is the passementerie, from the French word *passement* meaning lace. These elaborate buttons are richly decorated with silk or metallic threads and added sequins, pastes, foil, or pearls. The fabric is gathered tightly over a center disk of wood or bone and padded to add depth. The passementiers of France were a protected medieval guild, and their designs were often imitated by makers of metal buttons.

In contrast, the needlework skills of poor women and girls in the English county of Dorset were used at least as early as 1690 by Abraham Case, who invented a ring-shaped button covered by fine lace stitchery known as a Dorset button. The work provided them with a way of supplementing the family income, but the wages were very low. The industry continued in the area throughout the eighteenth century; the use of a metal ring was introduced in 1750 by Case's grandson Peter. The ring was covered with thread, and stitches were woven back and forth to create simple designs called Dorset crosswheel, cartwheel, or basketweave. Sometimes a second color was added around the edge of the buttons. Dorset buttons continued to be made in almost the same way for the next 150 years, so collectors will find supplies of these buttons, but may have difficulty determining the age.

··MACHINE-MADE FABRIC BUTTONS··

The coming of the Industrial Revolution would suggest the end of the cloth button since it was based on labor intensive handwork. However, in 1825 Benjamin Sanders Jr of Birmingham, England, improved the cloth-covered, metal-backed button with an iron shank patented by his father and developed the pad-backed button which protected the cloth of the garment from harsh edges of the metal shank. Mass production led to increased production of woven silk buttons.

BELOW
Eighteenth-century button makers constructed beautiful creations using gold and silver floss or fine silk embroidery on linen, or silk fabric drawn over a wooden form and gathered securely for men's fashions.

1. Floral and leaf pattern on silk with embroidered border; 1 in/2.5 cm; worn as part of a set on a gentleman's coat to match the fabric of the jacket; c 1780; French.
2. Called passementerie; 1¼ in/3 cm; probably the same type of embroidery as on jacket or to contrast with black silk coat; part of a set; c 1770; French.
3. Embroidered floral design with wreath border on linen; 1 in/2.5 cm; c 1780; French.
4. Floral sleeve or vest button; c 1780; French.

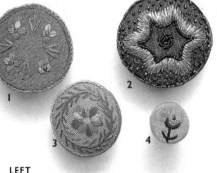

LEFT
Machine-embroidered buttons manufactured in France in the late nineteenth century for women's costumes imitated the work of the eighteenth-century button makers.

1. Conventional design in pastels on white silk fabric drawn on metal top and fitted into metal back to hold the fabric; metal loop shank; 1 in/2.5 cm.
2. Stylized floral pictorial with pink border on silk; 1 in/2.5 cm.
3. Light blue with silver floss to frame floral design in the center, on silk; metal back with loop shank; 1 in/2.5 cm.
4. Light pink spokes on white silk fabric; metal back; ¾ in/2 cm.
5. Black button – same design as 2; 1¼ in/3 cm; probably used on dress or jacket.

The supply is plentiful today, but collectors will find them very plain, following the fashion dictates of the day.

In the United States in 1834, Samuel Williston of Easthampton, Massachusetts, began the mechanical production of metal-backed fabric buttons. The business began with his wife's hand-sewn buttons, but soon the manufacture of metal-backed buttons, some with the trademark "Williston," was flourishing. These examples are highly sought by collectors, particularly those with the backmark described.

Woven materials made on jacquard looms, developed in 1801, were used for ribbons and buttons. French and English manufacturers set small designs of silk, velvet, wool, and other fabrics in metal frames. In 1867 Thomas Stevens of Coventry, England, established a company which made buttons and badges. His looms created woven pictures called textilographs, or Stevensgraphs by collectors. In the same area, JJ Cash started his ribbon firm in 1864; it also manufactured silk woven buttons and still produces designs today.

····COLLECTING FABRIC BUTTONS····

While fabric buttons are still available today and tailors and homesewers can make their own covered cloth buttons, their interest to collectors is primarily due to the picture on the fabric. Collectors are most interested in eighteenth and

LEFT
The decorative use of crochet or beading resulted in buttons that enhanced plain fabrics.

1. Crocheted top in off-white with added crocheted border; 1½ in/3.8 cm; England; c 1860.
2. Tan ball encased in crochet; ½ in/1.2 cm; c 1860.
3. 1 in/2.5 cm beaded rose design on linen; c 1880; drawn and gathered over wooden form; probably worn on evening fashion.
4. Star design crocheted over gray silk fabric; 1 in/2.5 cm; c 1880; French.
5 Conventional crocheted design over brown silk; 1 in/2.5 cm; c 1890.

LEFT

Black fabric buttons, like black glass, were manufactured in great quantity from 1861 on.

1. 1 in/2.5 cm button with cording and scalloped edges; pad back; *c* 1910.
2. Modern 1 in/2.5 cm velvet button with center glass jewel and gold and silver cording to form design; metal back and loop shank.
3. 1 in/2.5 cm evening coat button, *c* 1910; beads and sequins form paisley design on silk fabric drawn and gathered over wooden mold.
4. ⅝ in/2 cm beaded button on silk, drawn and gathered at the back over a mold.
5. Crocheted design on oval button to create a design with depth; pad back; *c* 1900.
6. Rectangular death's-head button with apex of four triangles meeting in the center; pad back; *c* 1900.
7. Brocade linen of flower; pad back.

nineteenth-century buttons, which show various types of construction and decoration. First come various handmade types, some beaded or embroidered. The fine details, the quality of the fabric, the detail of the picture, and the preservation of the button make these collectible. The artistry and age of highly sought passementerie buttons make them desirable. The last group of handmade buttons are the crocheted examples. A variety of stitches and techniques were used to form the button. Some were made by hand by cottage workers; later examples were also machine-crocheted.

One significant design in this handmade category is the Devil's Head, a strange name for a fabric button. Developed and produced by Williston, this pattern is sometimes called crochet because of the small stitches which form the rows that make up the four triangles which meet at the center. The bases of the triangles form the edge of the button, and their apexes meet in the middle. As the name implies, this type of button is usually black, but pastel shades and dark colors may be found.

The variety of decoration on fabric buttons provides collectors with a way to group their buttons. One popular group is the molded-top button which, as the name suggests, has a top which appears to be molded into a fabric design. The most desirable are pictorials like a leaf, an acorn, or a bell. These small buttons, usually half an inch in diameter, are often as high as they are round. They may be decorated with twist or other trim, and they are always found with the pad back

ABOVE

Called molded-tops or "Gone with the Wind," these buttons matched the fabric of ladies' dresses of the 1860s, and were among the first buttons used on women's fashions. The designs consisted of several pieces of cardboard, covered with cloth and decorated with cording. The pictorial designs are more desirable to collectors. All have pad backs and were sold in sets of 20–24 buttons, used in single or double rows to fasten or decorate the bodice of a dress.

BELOW
Fabric buttons of the mid to late
eighteenth century were decorated with
a variety of techniques and materials.

1. Velvet rim fitted into metal back with
pad back; 1¼ in/3 cm; c early twentieth
century.
2.,3. Silk buttons in pink and brown by
A Parent Cie.; c 1870; France.
4. Embroidered floral design on velvet,
drawn and gathered over wooden mold;
meant for woman's costume; 1 in/2.5 cm;
c 1860.
5. Black glass center with silver luster
mounted in metallic fabric frame with
pad back; worn on dress or jacket;
⅝ in/2 cm; c 1880.
6. Metal butterfly on silk; pad back;
worn on dress in sets of many buttons;
½ in/1.2 cm; c 1890.
7. Like 4. in construction, age, and
purpose; embroidered shamrock on
velvet.

invented by Sanders. Collectors also look for a variety of colors since they may be blue, pink, russet, yellow, and green. Probably they were among the first women's buttons which were more than decoration; they can be seen on gowns in Godey prints and on Scarlett O'Hara in *Gone With the Wind*.

Other center decorations interest collectors. Many buttons with pad backs have glass or metal centers and velvet borders set in a metal frame. The designs in the center are often pictorials like a basket, a person's head, or an animal. The glass may be black, clear, or colored. These centers are also found mounted in metal or other materials. Collectors can pair a fabric button with a metal one having the same center design.

Fabric, especially velvet, was used as a background for the desirable picture buttons of the Victorian era. Sometimes called "perfume buttons" (it is thought that the ladies saturated the buttons with perfume), they come in all sizes with many designs. Collectors can pair buttons with the velvet background with ones without the fabric.

Another type of decoration is the cut-out, in which the fabric shows through a design cut or punched in a piece of metal. The fabric may be velvet or, later, metallic woven

RIGHT
Perfume or velvet-back buttons, as well
as metallic strands, showed the use of
fabric as a background material for
picture buttons of the late nineteenth
century.

1. Called Mme Butterfly or Mme
Chrysanthemum. Off-white velvet
became the fabric behind the ribs of
parasols; 1¼ in/3.1 cm brass button with
japanned back and loop shank; c 1880;
European or English.
2. Brass button with original finish of
dark blue; japanned back with loop
shank; 1 in/2.5 cm; c 1890.
3. Metal escutcheon of woman's head in
brass frame with pad back; ¾ in/2 cm;
c 1870; probably worn on dress.
4. Fleur -de-lis design; ½ in/1.2 cm brass
button with japanned back with loop
shank; c 1880

ABOVE

An original Cash card shows how the woven buttons with the characteristic pad back were sold in sets in the twentieth century.

1.,2. Delicate floral patterns were woven or embroidered on silk to match the color of the dress or blouse; ⅝ in/1.6 cm; c 1920–1930.

3. Woven image of Queen Elizabeth II for her coronation in 1953; meant as lapel button like those for Queen Victoria.

4. Woven Union Jack ribbon, probably for the coronation in 1953.

ABOVE

Modern clowns designed for collectors by the Texas State Button Society, as favors for a national and a state meeting to celebrate the circus in the late 1980s, show the continuing use of fabric.

1. Hand embroidered; favor for **NBS** meeting in Dallas, 1990; metal back with loop shank; fabric drawn over metal plate and fitted into the back; ¾ in/2 cm.

2. Painted clown on fabric with plastic shank applied; collar and hair glued to the original button.

LEFT AND BELOW

Garter buttons of the 1920s showed the flapper or the policeman saying "STOP!" on printed silk or satin buttons.

1. Ribbons covered the metal garter; metal back and loop shank; ⅝ in/2 cm; **USA.**

2. Printed fabric with large eyes, drawn and gathered over a wooden form with a ribbon ruff added on the back of the button; 1 in/2.5 cm; **USA.**

3. Policeman; pad back; ⅝ in/1.6 cm; **USA.**

4. Detailed printed fabric with rose in left corner; pad back; ⅝ in/1.6 cm; **USA.**

5.,6. Metal back and loop shank; ⅝ in/1.6 cm; **USA.**

ribbon. These inexpensive examples are often a good starting place for the beginning collector of fabric buttons.

Machine woven buttons made by the companies mentioned before are valuable in a collection. Stevens buttons are rare, so they are highly collectible. Cash buttons, with the floral designs of the nineteenth century and designs for coronations and jubilees of various British monarchs, provide more fabric pictorials. In the early twentieth century, fabrics were printed with likenesses of Betty Boop and other flappers to be used as garter buttons. On one, a policeman signaled "STOP!" to whoever might venture beyond the garter. These modern buttons have become very desirable and expensive.

Fabric buttons are fragile, and their plainness has sometimes made them less desirable to collectors. Since they can be overlooked – except for the most outstanding eighteenth-century ones – a beginning collector can start with cloth buttons as a way to learn about construction, decoration, and design. Collectors of fabric buttons should look for all types of the buttons described and for a variety of colors. It is easy to find plain, black buttons. Finding others is more difficult.

METAL BUTTONS

CHAPTER 3

Buttons can be found in a variety of metals, including copper, steel, brass, pewter, silver, aluminum, and tin. Many were stamped in dies, while others were engraved or chased, with the design stamped by hand into a flat button. The variety of metal buttons is endless – from the early copper buttons of the eighteenth century with geometric and conventional, nonpictorial designs to the many Victorian metal buttons showing people, animals, objects, and stories. Although these buttons are not as exquisite as some other types, such as enamel, many collectors choose to specialize in metal because of the variety of different materials, and the subject matter and intricacy of detail found on these buttons.

················ COPPER BUTTONS ················

Some of the finest metal buttons ever made were the copper buttons made during the last three decades of the eighteenth century. Large buttons were the fashion; coat buttons averaged 1½in/3.5cm in diameter, and sleeve, waistcoat, and breeches buttons measured 1in/2.5cm. Most were flat with a thick half-round shank fastened on with solder. Because copper tarnishes easily, the buttons were often finished by gilding, painting, or engraving. The painting was not fired on and wore off in use, although some buttons have been preserved in their original condition, so we know what they looked like. Decorations included enamel plaques, jasperware medallions, or paintings on ivory under glass. Most of these buttons were made in Birmingham, England, for export to France, the largest consumer. The fancier buttons were rarely made in smaller sizes, which are commonly found with stamped or engraved, conventional designs. Large buttons began to go out of fashion around the beginning of the nineteenth century when Beau Brummell adopted a dark-colored coat with plain gilt buttons. The die was cast for men's fashion – it was no longer the showy plumage of male birds, but the somber male garb that is still in fashion today. The large copper buttons of the late eighteenth century, especially those with decorations, are rare and expensive.

In the mid eighteenth century, steel works were established in England by men like **Matthew Boulton**, who developed a process to create buttons to imitate silver and to massproduce these for the button trade.

1. Openwork in the typical 36 mm size, with cut steel trim and heavy steel shank.
2. Steel combined with pearl, fabric, and paste trim and a heavy steel shank.
3. Flat steel disk with cut steel in the center and beveled edge; heavy steel shank.
4. Nineteenth century steel, c 1830, with stamped design in flat disk; 1 in/2.5 cm; steel shank. For men's coats or vests.

RIGHT

Cut steel buttons of the late nineteenth century were constructed of faceted pieces that were riveted or soldered to a plain base. Openwork designs, a variety of shapes, and the intricate patterns make these lighter steel buttons with wire shanks very collectible.

LEFT

Large copper buttons which were hand-stamped, punched, or incised with a design were in fashion on men's clothing in sets of 20–24 buttons in the late eighteenth century. Often called "copper colonials," plain buttons like these were also highly decorated with enamels, pastes, and jasperware disks.

STEEL BUTTONS

Steel, a mixture of iron and carbon, is another material commonly found on buttons. It was used both as a base and as decoration. Because it rusts rapidly in the presence of water or moisture in the air, it does not seem like a suitable material for buttons. Nevertheless, many buttons of highly polished steel or other materials trimmed with steel were manufactured in the late eighteenth century and throughout the nineteenth century.

Large steel buttons were popular along with copper buttons during the last three decades of the eighteenth century. The most famous maker of steel buttons was Matthew Boulton of Birmingham, who included jasperware plaques from Wedgwood in some of his buttons, now prized by collectors.

Steel buttons for women's fashions became popular during the nineteenth century. The best of these consist of hundreds of tiny, faceted steel pieces (also known as "cut steels") riveted onto brass or steel backs. Cheap substitutes made by simple stamping of a sheet of steel to imitate separately applied pieces were also manufactured, but close examination shows that the pieces are not riveted to the back. Cut steel was sometimes dyed red, blue, or green, and pieces in several colors were used on one button. Flat steel buttons were also sometimes decorated with color.

Another type of steel button is made of a saucer-shaped steel disk with a decorative center of a different material, such

as glass, pearl, other metal, or enamel. These are commonly called "steel cups." Collectors can look for these buttons in small, medium, and large sizes and try to find a variety of different centers.

Many steel buttons have survived, but they rarely show the brilliance they once had. A button is definitely made of steel if it can be picked up with a magnet. Steel buttons should be handled as little as possible because of their tendency to rust. Once steel has rusted, it is impossible to restore the luster. Unless the button is rare, the collector should be selective in buying steel buttons that show signs of rust.

·········· P E W T E R   B U T T O N S ··········

Pewter is the generic term for an alloy of tin and other metals, the composition of which can vary. The best pewter was thought to contain at least 90 percent tin. Pewter was commonly used in the late eighteenth and early nineteenth centuries to make buttons for men's clothing. The first pewter buttons were made in molds and had a self shank, but because pewter is a soft metal the shanks frequently broke off. A pewter button with an iron shank was introduced by the Grilley brothers of Waterbury, Connecticut, in about 1800. After this, the name of the manufacturer often appeared on the back of the button.

Pewter buttons made in America in the early nineteenth century were called "hard white" by their makers, probably to distinguish them from the cheap low-grade buttons used by the working classes. The patterns on many of the hard whites were the same as those on steel buttons, and in some cases the buttons were even stamped "Imitation Steel." Face patterns are usually conventional, and star and pinwheel patterns are commonly found. Small one-piece pewter vest buttons with a separately applied rim of brass were also manufactured during this period, but are scarce. In about 1810, pewterers began to shift to making brass buttons, and by the 1830s brass buttons had replaced the hard whites.

In the last half of the nineteenth century, pewter appeared again as a material for buttons, this time for ladies' wear. Many of these buttons have stamped or cast designs tinted with varnish and enhanced by bright cutting, thus giving rise to the

ABOVE
Buttons with a shallow steel cup with a raised rim may be decorated in the centers with a variety of materials and were manufactured in the late nineteenth century when picture buttons were very popular.

1. Pewter background with brass figure of a soldier added; wire metal shank; 1 in/2.5 cm.
2. Stamped vegetable ivory with an escutcheon made from a thin sheet of brass.
3. Turned wood decorated with cut steels in the center of the steel cup.
4. Green celluloid with large cut steel decorating the center.
5. Cut steel blades held on by a cut steel trim spin on a brass windmill.

BELOW
Pewter buttons were stamped and
tinted in the late nineteenth century to
be used on women's clothing.

1.,2.,3.,4.,6. Tinted pewter with bright
cut designs showing floral patterns;
colors would match the fabric.
3.,4. Shank molded with the button.
5. Tinted button called bright cut
pewter with design cut through the dye
to twinkle out.

name for these buttons – "tinted bright cut pewters." These pewter buttons are common today, and a group of them with various designs and in various colors makes a nice display.

Pewter buttons continue to be made in various shapes and sizes. They are more finely crafted than many other mass-produced modern buttons, and a collector could assemble a nice assortment of modern pewter buttons.

················· **BRASS BUTTONS** ·················

Brass, an alloy of copper and zinc, has been used to manufacture more buttons than any other material. With the advent of mass production methods during the later part of the eighteenth century, brass became a popular material for buttons. Brass ingots were rolled between steel rollers and button blanks by the thousand were stamped from the thin sheets of brass. Factory workers added preformed wire shanks and a bit of solder, which melted when the buttons were heated in ovens. By 1820, the two-piece button, consisting of two stamped metal shells making the front and back and folded tightly at the rim, replaced the older one-piece type. Most of these buttons have conventional or floral designs.

The early brass buttons were all made in England, but by the 1830s several American firms had acquired the knowledge to compete with the British. The American industry was centered in New England, and manufacturers included Scovills, Benedict & Burnham, and Robinsons. The peak of production of these American buttons was between 1830 and 1850, and buttons from this period are often called "Golden Age" because of their high quality. Many have backmarks; one way to collect these buttons is to hunt for different backmarks.

During the 1830s, some small brass waistcoat buttons, typically ½in/1.3cm to ¾in/2cm in size and characterized by a separate rim added to the one-piece body, were made. The designs on many of these buttons reflect the patriotism of the era. David F Johnson coined the name "Jacksonian," after Andrew Jackson, who was President at the time. Typical subjects were squirrels, eagles, deer, baskets, flowers, and anchors. Over one hundred patterns have been listed, but many are very scarce. Similar buttons having conventional rather than pictorial designs are referred to as Jacksonian

BELOW
American gilt buttons of the 1830–1840 period used in gentlemen's clothing are called "Golden Age" buttons and were backmarked with the maker's name; collectors seek pictorials and conventional designs, as well as hand-chased buttons.

BELOW
Small pictorial vest buttons, about ½ in/1.2 cm in size with separate rims, were manufactured in the United States in the 1825–1840 period. They are called Jacksonians after Andrew Jackson, the President at that time (1.,4.,5.,6. and 8.); a Jacksonian cousin is manufactured in the same way but has a conventional, rather than a pictorial, design. (2.,3. and 7.).

"cousins." They are also scarce, but not as desirable as the pictorial Jacksonians.

Brass buttons decorated with sporting subjects were also made in this period and worn by sporting enthusiasts. Sporting buttons were usually made with several related designs to a set, frequently six or more. Typical designs depicted game animals or hunters.

After 1850, the quality of gilt buttons began to decline, and in the 1860s stamped brass picture buttons began to appear for women's and children's wear. Most are two-piece with a lacquered steel back and are collected for their interesting subject matter rather than because they are made of brass.

Brass buttons covered with a varnish imitating lacquer are called "japanned" brass. These buttons with their black backgrounds and painted designs resemble the toleware that was popular in the eighteenth and nineteenth centuries. Most are concave or convex, and floral designs in colored paint or monochrome scenes with white on the black background are common. On some, the only decoration is created by engraving through the background to show a brass outline of the design.

SILVER BUTTONS

Although silver buttons were probably made in the sixteenth and seventeenth centuries, the collector will find it almost impossible to find buttons made before the middle of the eighteenth century. Silver buttons have been made in many countries, and a wide variety can be collected.

British silver has been hallmarked since the late thirteenth century, so if a hallmark is found, it is possible to date the button within a year or two. Unfortunately, silversmiths of the eighteenth and early nineteenth centuries did not bother to hallmark their small buttons. Since the mid-1800s when silver buttons came into fashion, most buttons have been hallmarked. American silver carries only the maker's mark or the word *sterling*, if anything.

Most solid silver buttons were made from sheets of silver stamped with designs; cast silver buttons were heavy and impractical. Most silver buttons from the eighteenth century are large, like the copper and steel buttons of the era, because they were made for men's coats. The few small ones found were made for breeches or are cuff buttons with the connecting links removed. Perhaps the oldest silver buttons the collector will find are large link buttons, which have regulation shanks with links attached. These were worn on peasant costumes to fasten the trousers to the shirt.

Silver buttons are always sought by collectors. Many examples of silver buttons from the nineteenth and early twentieth centuries can be found, but their quality varies greatly. Designs commonly found on these buttons are flowers, horses, women, children, couples, and cherubs. Many of the better buttons were sold in boxed sets of six. Some were decorated with enameling, especially basse-taille (see Chapter 6.) Many examples with an Art Nouveau style can be found. There were also some beautiful silver and enameled buttons imported from the Far East.

Niello is a technique used in making silver buttons. The lines of the design are cut in a disk of silver, which is then completely covered with a black composition material. Next, the disk is subjected to heat. When the button cools, the top surface is scraped and burnished, leaving the black composition in the design lines. Nineteenth-century niello buttons are scarce, but those from the 1940s can be found, most made in Thailand for export and marked "Sterling, made in Siam."

American Indian silver is another category of button sought by the collector. The Navaho were taught to work with silver in the 1850s by a Mexican and spread the art to the Zuni. Both

BELOW

Silver buttons, worn from the sixteenth century on, are more readily available to collectors from the twentieth century.

1.,2.,3.,4. Hallmarked British silver buttons. Obvious influence of the Art Nouveau movement; sold in sets of six–eight.

5. Navaho Indian silver with coral decoration of southwestern United States. Many were made for tourists in the 1940s and 1950s, and are still made today in small quantities. This one from c 1980.

6. Niello work done in Thailand from 1945–49; marked Sterling, made in Siam; engraved into blackened silver; heart shape showing temple dancer.

7. Japanese enameled silver showing a wisteria in openwork design; Japanese backmark; early twentieth century.

tribes used turquoise in their silverwork. Interest in Indian art during the first three decades of the twentieth century led to commercialization of Indian crafts to satisfy tourist demands.

Handmade Indian silver buttons are rarely found today, except in private collections. However, many examples of fine craftsmanship can still be found today. Because they were made in so many forms and designs, there is no limit to the number and types of Indian silver buttons that can be collected.

ALUMINUM BUTTONS

Because aluminum is always found in combined form and is expensive to isolate and because it was not as attractive as silver, it was never used extensively for buttons. A few beautiful aluminum buttons were made during the Victorian period, but these are scarce. In the 1930s and '40s, an aluminum stencil was introduced, which was claimed to be more durable than the china stencils used at the time. A base coat of enamel or paint was applied, followed by the stencil design, and a final coat of lacquer, with baking after each step. The stencil designs imitated those found on china buttons, but were not as varied. However, the color range was large. Contrary to the advertisement for these buttons, the lacquer did not hold up well, and not many are found in good condition, but they are interesting finds for a collector.

TIN BUTTONS

Tin is a soft, silvery-white metal. Because it does not tarnish readily and is nontoxic, it is used as a protective coating on other metals. Tin-plated sheet iron has been used extensively for buttons, principally for the backs. "Tin" buttons is a term applied to certain late nineteenth century two-piece buttons that were made of a dull gray metal, identified as zinc, coated with tin. Once the coating is gone, the metal cannot be polished. Many Victorian picture buttons were made of this material, and it was also used for rims of buttons.

ABOVE
Aluminum stencilled buttons were manufactured in bright colors from 1930–40 by the Patent Button Company and the Atlas Tack Company, in a process in which several coats of enamel were baked onto the aluminum and the final stencil design was added.

BELOW RIGHT
Brass and pewter picture buttons of the late nineteenth century provide collectors with pictorials of objects, animals and birds, plant life, and people in intricately designed metal work.

1. Grand Canal of Venice with the St Marks spire; brass; 1½ in; japanned back.
2. Cupid with bow on screen-like background with handkerchief border; brass; 1½ in/3.8 cm; japanned back.
3. Mme Butterfly; stamped brass with ink-substance added to highlight design; japanned back; 1 in/2.5 cm.
4. Stamped design of cranes with original red tint; western rendition of Oriental theme; japanned back; 1½ in/3.8 cm.
5. One-piece stamped pewter button of water lily; ½ in/1.2 cm.
6. Back of woman with a fan, with tinting to give color to her costume; japanned back; 1½ in/3.8 cm.

········ METAL PICTURE BUTTONS ········

All buttons with designs other than conventional or geometric ones are classified as picture buttons. The range of subjects is endless – flowers, animals, architectural scenes, dragons, cupids, fairies, fables, music, drama, heads, mythology, games, transportation, stories, oriental themes, to name only a few. A popular way for collectors to group picture buttons is by subject.

More picture buttons were made of metal than of any other material. The designs were repeated over the years and by many different manufacturers. The first metal picture buttons were made in the mid-nineteenth century, and many more were made by the end of the century.

Picture buttons with designs depicting identifiable myths, fables, nursery rhymes, operas, etc., are called story buttons. Although many picture buttons suggest stories, only those that can be identified by the illustrations qualify as story buttons. Some examples of recognizable stories found on buttons are: nursery rhymes – Jack and Jill, Little Bo Peep, and Mary Had a Little Lamb; children's stories – Little Red Riding Hood, Sleeping Beauty, and Buster Brown and Tige; drama and opera – *Romeo and Juliet*, Sarah Bernhardt, *Carmen*, and *Rigoletto*; mythology – Neptune, Achilles, and Minerva; fables – the fox and the grapes, the milkmaid and her pail, and the fox and the crow; biblical stories – St Christopher, Moses in the Bulrushes, and St Cecilia at the Organ.

Story buttons are some of the most desired buttons by collectors. It is satisfying to identify the designs with stories, and there are many story buttons that are plentiful and easily found. The rarer story buttons command high prices.

ABOVE
Popular story buttons cause collectors to match narratives with buttons created during the heyday of the picture button, the 1880–1900 period.

1. One-piece stamped brass top of **Man Friday** from novel *Robinson Crusoe* by Defoe; japanned back; 1 in/2.5 cm.
2. Stamped button called "Tom Sawyer" or "Loitering After School;" japanned back; 1 in/2.5 cm.
3. "Red Riding Hood and the Wolf" in stamped brass with white metal collet; japanned back; 1 in/2.5 cm.
4. "Little Bo Peep," after the Kate Greenaway illustration; tin background with brass design; white metal collet; japanned back; 1 in/2.5 cm.
5. "King Arthur" in brass center design on square with fabulous animal border; Paris backmark.
6. "Farewell to Frederique," from Goethe; stamped brass in japanned back; 1½ in/3.8 cm.
7. "Pied Piper of Hamlin" with figure in bright brass over blackened background of the village; 2 in/5 cm.
8 "Blondel," musician of Richard I, singing to find his master; stamped brass; japanned back; 1½ in/3.8 cm.

Glass Buttons

PATENT

Collecting glass buttons is an excellent way to begin. Glass buttons are plentiful, so beginning collectors have many to specialize in. Many small buttons are available, and large pictorials in both colored and black glass are very desirable. Certainly, no other medium illustrates so well the idea that buttons imitate, since imitation fabric, wood, gemstones, and metal are available in glass.

····· CLEAR AND COLORED GLASS ·····

The earliest glass beads, found in the Mediterranean area, date to 4000 BC. European glassmakers were established as early as 1226, and buttons were being made by the fifteenth century. They were thick disks of glass, many with faceted edges, with a pinshank inserted in the center. Few survive, and it is very difficult to differentiate them from similar ones made through the eighteenth century.

The heyday of glass buttonmaking ran from 1840 to 1918, but glass buttons continued to be produced into the early 1960s. Traditionally, the region near Gablonz, Czechoslovakia, called Bohemia, as well as regions of Austria, Germany, and France, are associated with glass buttons. As metal "Golden Age" buttons declined in popularity, the glass button was used by tailors and fashion designers. Many buttons of the 1840s were called "swirlbacks." Glassmakers made a swirl on the back of the molded buttons before cutting off the glass, and a simple metal shank or a metal staple shank was inserted into the hot glass. They are found with a variety of trims and decorations in all colors including black. Glass overlays and glass trims applied during manufacturing added second colors or designs. Metal designs were embedded into a hot button, and thread or metal strips were used to bind the cooled button. Steel trim, paste trims, foil or paper backs, or paint were also added after the button cooled. Young girls kept charm strings of buttons before their marriages, hoping to find 999 different buttons; their fiancé added the 1,000th button. Nowadays it is more difficult to find old charm strings than it used to be; most have been taken apart so the buttons could be sold individually.

Not all old glass buttons were swirlbacks, and the types are classified by collectors according to their manufacture or trim.

Paperweight buttons, found in old and modern glass, are constructed just like desk weights, and some old ones were swirlbacks. A base is formed and a design of canes or foil added. Then the colored base is covered with a dome of clear glass which can be decorated after cooling. Companies manufactured these buttons before 1918 in France, Britain, and the United States. After 1918 some were made in Italy and Czechoslovakia, and studio button makers such as Charles Kazin, Thure Erickson, Robert Banford, Theresa Rarig, John Gooderham, and others have made paperweights for button collectors. Paperweight buttons are among the most expensive glass buttons, especially the modern studio ones.

Radiant glass buttons are the opposite of swirlbacks; they were molded of clear glass on the top and back with tiny dots of a second color dropped into the design. More rarely, the body of the button is colored glass, especially yellow or greenish-yellow. One group of radiants has a dot of color at the shank. The color reflects through the molded tops, which may be very elaborate. Called reflectors, they are the most common radiants. Another radiant is the dewdrop, which has a clear molded top and a molded back with ribs or spokes in which tiny dots of color are placed. The third type is the glory, named for the morning glory which it resembled. Its molded smooth dome top had a fluted or ridged conical back, and color was tipped in at the shank. These fragile buttons command high prices.

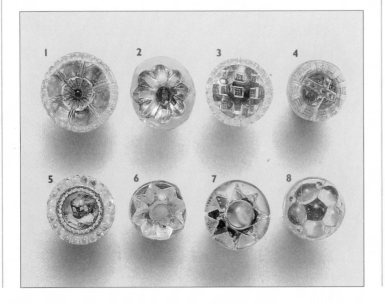

RIGHT
Paperweights, formed with a base color and a set-up design, are usually encased in a top of clear glass; all three parts are essential for the button to be a true paperweight.

1. Modern; ⅝ in/1.5 cm.
2. ½ in/1.7 cm; probably German, c 1950s; imported to fabric stores for use on children's clothing.
3. Purple base with bubble design; may be Charles Kaziun; c 1970 for collectors.
4. Gold butterfly of foil on blue base in clear cap; a design made popular by Kaziun; 1970s for collectors.
5. Square made by John Gooderham; late 1980s for collectors; ¾ in/2 cm.
6. White base with goldstone and center rose design; typical design used by old and modern paperweight makers; ⅝ in/1.5 cm ball.
7. Green conventional design on a pink base; modern, made in Czechoslovakia and imported for collectors.
8. Square with pinched clear top; type made by Weinman; ¾ in/2 cm; 1960s.

LEFT
Small glass buttons with glass drops added as trim are called radiants but are distinguished as glories, dewdrops, and reflectors.

1.,3.,4.,5.,8. Called reflectors, with molded tops and glass applied at the metal shank to reflect design through the top; one drop of color adds all the color design because of the top and back molding in the glass; probably used on men's vests or women's clothing; ½–⅝ in/1.2–1.5 cm; c 1850.
2.,6. Called glories, in which dome at top is plain and design is molded on the back with color drop added at the inserted metal shank; similar to a flower; ½–⅝ in/1.2–1.5 cm; c 1850.
7. Called a dewdrop, with several drops of glass in circle, usually around the molded back design, to represent drops of dew on the glass. Larger than most radiants, with molded top design also; ⅝ in/1.5 cm; c 1850.

BELOW

Kaleidoscope buttons are characterized by a foil design which reflects through a plain or molded top and is protected by a tin back with a loop shank. All are ⅝ in/1.5cm; probably USA. Worn on men's vests; c 1840–1860.

Kaleidoscope glass buttons are metal backed. A sheet of tin with a loop shank covers the back and allows the clear or colored molded tops to be decorated. A foil sheet placed between the glass top and the tin back gave the effect of looking through a kaleidoscope. Sometimes the back of the button was mirrored, and the top, available in many colors, was etched with a pictorial design. Some metal backs served as a base into which pieces of glass, similar to beads, were riveted. Paper also was glued to the back of molded tops, and these are called paperbacks.

One of the most expensive glass buttons is the Tingue, made in three parts. A molded base, in a ball, square, rectangular, or round shape, has a faceted design. A piece of foil lines a groove or pocket in the top of the base, and a dot of red or blue glass is added. A top of clear glass protects the foil compartment. Many have self-shanks, but occasionally a plate and loop shank is found.

The most plentiful glass buttons are the ones with molded pictorial designs. Hot glass was added to metal molds stamped to look like metal picture buttons. Often the glass was opaque. Various finishes decorated the button. Lusters created from various metallic compounds gave the button an iridescent, silver, or gold appearance. Some dealers call the finish "carnival" after the carnival glass popular with collectors of glassware. None of the companies which made carnival glassware is known to have made buttons, but the finish is

RIGHT

Tingue buttons from 1850–60 are among the most desirable and collectible of glass buttons. They are very fragile, due to their construction of an opaque or translucent base in colored or black glass with a piece of foil, a piece of red or blue glass, and a clear glass top which is cemented as a protection. All buttons here show the variety of design.

RIGHT

Molded pictorial glass buttons became fashionable in the 1880s and more so later with the rise in popularity of the metal picture buttons.

1. Domed orange glass depicting bee in a hive; cone shank with metal loop similar to those found on hatpins; probably used on women's coats or cloaks; 1¼ in/ 3.2 cm; c 1900.

2. Cone shank in black glass with bat and star design; popular in the **Art Nouveau** period.

3. Blue glass with white paint on conventional design; 2 in/5 cm, with cone shank.

4. Molded glass floral design; ¾ in/2 cm; Art Nouveau influence in "looping" design; with four-way metal box shank. Used on women's dresses or costumes c 1910–1918. Called "Victorians" by collectors.

5.,6. Art Nouveau 1 in/2.5 cm buttons, c 1910. Used on women's dresses or on summer costumes.

7. Molded "Victorian."

similar. Paint was sometimes used to highlight parts of the design. Decorative transfers, like those used in ceramics, were also applied to buttons. Some glass buttons even look like wood.

Lacy glass buttons, in small, medium, and large sizes, have a delicate molded face which looks like a lace design. A design painted on the back of the button often gives the clear glass the appearance of color. The back was then overpainted with a black or metallic paint to protect the first coat. While clear glass is used most frequently, colored glass in amber, blue, red, and green have been found. Usually these buttons have a metal loop and plate shank or a four-way box shank. Since they are fragile, buttons in perfect condition command high prices.

LEFT

Lacy glass buttons of the late nineteenth century were molded clear glass with a paint or transfer design applied to the back. This was protected with metallic paint and sealed with black paint so the design colored the button. All the buttons here were made in the same way. They are usually ¾–1¼ in/2–3.2 cm. They have a plate and loop shank or four-way metal box shanks, and are similar to Sandwich glass made in the US, but probably made in Bohemia with other glass of the period.

BLACK GLASS

When Prince Albert died in 1861, Queen Victoria went into mourning. The world followed, and the black glass industry reached its height of production. The queen's mourning jewelry and buttons were made of jet, a lightweight, highly fragile, and expensive mineral mined in Whitby in north-east England. True jet buttons are rare, but from 1861 until 1900, black glass makers, primarily in Bohemia and Austria, made tons of buttons using the same techniques and designs as for clear and colored glass. These buttons are called "jet," but are black glass meant to imitate the Queen's jet.

MODERN GLASS

After World War I, glassmakers, many of German descent, re-established their factories in Czechoslovakia with some success. Then, in 1939, Hitler invaded the area, which he called the Sudetenland, and the industry collapsed again. With the establishment of the Marshall Plan in 1946 and the movement of many Sudeten German glassmakers to Bavaria and the settlement at Neugablonz, an industry developed which produced highly collectible glass buttons. From the late 1940s to the early 1960s, shiploads of West German glass buttons flowed into Europe and the United States, and collectors could buy bright-colored glass buttons in fabric stores.

In addition to the small and medium molded and painted pictorial buttons, the glassmakers developed the "moonglow."

LEFT
With the death of her husband Albert in 1861, Queen Victoria went into mourning, and black became *the* fashion color of the end of the nineteenth century; glass makers created black glass buttons, often called "jet" to describe their color rather than their material, in designs to match the fabric of the clothing.

1. Used for women's costumes; 1 1/4 in/ 3.2 cm with four-way metal box shank, *c* 1910
2. Formerly called passementerie after the fabric buttons of the eighteenth century, faceted pieces of glass are soldered or riveted in place in a metal openwork frame; 3/4 in/2 cm.
3. Molded women's head in Art Nouveau design with four-way metal box shank, *c* 1900.
4. Paint applied to molded black glass to simulate moire fabric. 1 in/2.5 cm; plate and loop shank.
5. Flat top with Nailsea design, and plate and loop shank; 5/8 in/4.2 cm.
6. Openwork molded button with leaf design; plate and loop shank; 5/8 in/ 4.2 cm; *c* 1880.
7. Swirlback shows use of colored glass by manufacturers as the fashion to black was becoming popular; 5/8 in/4.2 cm; *c* 1870.
8. Square with white glass overlay sheet on black base; plate and loop shank.
9. Realistic horseshoe design; *c* 1885.
10. Square with enameled flowers; plate and loop shank.

In this button an opaque base topped with a thin, clear glass overlay gives the illusion of a swirl or eye in the center when the button is viewed from above. Some buttons were molded to create a pictorial which might then have been painted or lustered. Some were decorated with clear or colored pastes; others had pierced designs. Moonglows, most often found in ½in/1.3cm, ⅝in/1.5cm and ¾in/2cm diameters, were made in all the rainbow colors as well as black and white. These highly collectible buttons are escalating in value, especially the rare pictorial and the pierced designs.

The variety of West German glass buttons is great. Some buttons, called aurora, have an iridescent luster finish found on moonglows, opaque pictorials, and molded transparent glass. Another type of glass button has a design formed under the smooth surface. Patterns include conventional pictorials, such as a sailing sloop, a woman's profile, and a bunch of grapes, and "candy stripes," in which stripes of color cross the opaque colored body of the button.

BELOW
Modern glass manufactured after World War II in Bavaria, Germany, became very popular in the 1950s and 1960s as the glass makers who had lived in Czechoslovakia started the industry and exported tons of buttons.

1.,5.,6. Called moonglows, with molded opaque glass topped with a clear glass overlay sheet. Sold in fabric stores for home sewing; ⅝ in/1.6 cm.
2. Clear molded glass sew-through with green paint on the reverse. 1940s design.
3. Metallic painted back to look like a mirror; self-shank; ⅝ in/1.6 cm.
4. Molded gray glass with cameo design of woman's head; ¾ in/2 cm.
7. Realistic hat in green glass with red bow painted on; self-shank.
8. Molded green glass of sailboat with blue water painted on; self-shank; ⅝ in/1.6 cm.

The artistry and the color of these modern glass buttons did not survive modern wash days. Plastic buttons were less breakable than the fragile glass ones, and by the late 1960s, few glass buttons were imported. Some stock sat in warehouses until recently, when collectors' demands called them out of storage.

Another type of modern glass button was created in England after World War II by a Czechoslovakian immigrant who settled near London and began the Bimini Glass Company. Large blobs of opaque colored or black glass were impressed with a coin or other metal object, often with a classical design. A loop shank with the company's name and logo (a bush in a pot) was glued to the back of the button. The pictorial designs are the most collectible, but conventional patterns and roughly molded designs are available. Another English glass company that produced similar post-war glass buttons was the English Glass Company (Englass) of Leicester which hired Czechoslovakian immigrants in the late 1940s.

·············· MOUNTED IN METAL ··············

Collectors regard glass set in a metal frame in a different class from other glass. Often the same design can be mounted in a frame and unmounted with an inserted shank. Often, these mounted buttons are less expensive and, when displayed, are quite beautiful. One desirable type of glass-in-metal button is the "Gay '90s" button with its large jewel-like glass center mounted in an intricate metal frame which often shows a Celtic influence in the design. These large buttons were used as cloak buttons in the late nineteenth century. Small plain or molded glass centers were set in frames and used as vests buttons throughout the nineteenth century. If the button has an elongated shank, it is called a "waistcoat" or vest button. If it has a small round eye shank, it is called a "small jewel" button. Companies in Europe and the United States, particularly the Chesire Manufacturing Company, made many of these still-plentiful buttons.

Small pieces of glass were used to form a design, mounted in a metal button frame, called "mosaics." Made mainly in Italy, mosaic buttons depict human figures, animals, birds, insects, flowers, and classical structures and are found in small, medium, and large sizes. The use of mosaics in buttons began in the 1830s and reached a peak of popularity around 1880, and modern mosaics are valued by collectors. It is said that the older the mosaic, the smoother the top of the button, and most modern ones do feel rough to the touch.

BELOW
Among immigrants from Czechoslovakia to England after World War II were a number of glass manufacturers who influenced the design of buttons in the English Glass Company and the Bimini Company during the 1950s.

1.,2.,4.,5. Bimini buttons with the characteristic stamping of the design on a blob of glass.
3. Molded design made by Englass – the English Glass Company – with self-shank. Other designs are found in transparent glass without luster.

RIGHT

Glass disks mounted in metal frames increased the use of glass in buttons and provided more durable buttons for clothing from the 1870s to modern times.

1. Molded black glass with silver luster to simulate lacy fabric in brass frame; 1 in/2.5 cm; *c* 1880.

2. Called a "Gay 90s button." Probably used in capes and coats *c* 1910–1920. German manufacture; 1½–2 in/3.8–5 cm; characterized by a large glass "stone" center in the metal frame.

3. Black glass center in metal frame, *c* 1870.

4. Two pieces of molded glass set in intricate design, *c* 1890.

5. Glass cover over paper design, often called "design under glass"; ¾ in/2 cm; *c* 1930.

6. Opaque Art Nouveau head, *c* 1890.

7. Stippled white opaque glass with painted floral design in brass frame; 1 in/2.5 cm, *c* 1900.

BELOW

Mosaics made in Italy were used in button manufacturing from 1830 on, and were available to tourists into the 1960s.
Center 6 Buttons: micro mosaics popular for use as men's vest buttons in the nineteenth century; usually a black base with classical scenes (2.,3.,6.); 1 incorporates use of goldstone in conventional design; floral in 4.,5. is common but use of pink and the oval design is unusual; mounting is often on low carat gold or gold wash on silver; ½ in/1.3 cm.
Outer 2 (7.,8.): More modern without the smoothness of earlier mosaic buttons; floral or conventional designs mounted in brass; *c* 1930s and later.

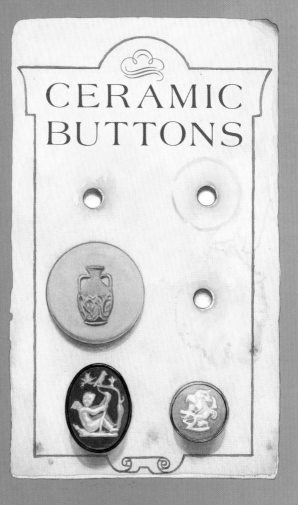

CERAMIC BUTTONS

A ceramic button, like any other piece made by a potter, is the result of mixing clay with water, adding other minerals if desired, forming the item, and baking or firing it in an oven or kiln. Early potters closely guarded the secrets which made their products different – the amount of water, the minerals added, the length and heat of the firing, even the source of the clay. For centuries, the Chinese tried to prevent their techniques from reaching the European world, but the knowledge finally made its way westward, and great factories were established in France, Germany, Holland, Italy, and England in the seventeenth and eighteenth centuries – just in time for use in the golden age of buttons. Neither the fashionable person nor a collector would be satisfied with an unglazed clay button, so the methods of decoration were very important. It is the decoration which makes a button collectible and differentiates factory from factory.

The earliest Western ceramics were earthenware, a porous clay made non-porous only when sealed with a glaze. The first step was the firing at a high temperature to dry the clay. Then the glaze was applied, and the item was fired again at a lower temperature. Each subsequent firing, as each decoration was applied one at a time, required another firing at lower temperatures. Each firing increased the possibility that the item would be lost. Despite this, *majolica* developed in Spain, *faience* in France, and *delft* in Holland. A few eighteenth-century pin-shank buttons, with floral decorations around the border and the metal knob of a pin placed through the ceramic disk and bent into a loop shank, are available. They illustrate the use of soft paste, an opaque ceramic fired at a much lower temperature than porcelain, and represent the first attempts to duplicate what the Chinese had discovered. In 1707 Ehrenfried Walter von Tschirnhaus developed *porcelain*, a non-porous, translucent body. This was the secret the Chinese had been protecting; the addition of minerals such as kaolin, feldspar, or quartz hardened the ceramic ware.

LEFT
The Zia Indians in the southwestern United States created brick-colored earthenware painted with rich colors of their tribal symbols throughout the 1940s.

In the late eighteenth century, soft-paste, self-shank ceramic buttons were glazed, decorated with floral motifs, and refired creating sets of buttons worn on men's coats and vests.

1. White button, painted with turquoise in ribbon pattern with gold edges and a floral design added; self-shank; 1¼ in/3.2 cm, c 1790.
2.,3. Basketweave molded ceramic button in 1 in/2.5 cm and ½ in/1.3 cm sleeve or vest size; self-shank; floral motif painted over the glaze; c 1790.

BELOW
Josiah Wedgwood found buttons to be a perfect medium for showing off his ceramic jasperware disks, and his factory mounted the disks in steel. The firm continues to make buttons today for special orders and for collectors.

1. Modern, c 1970s, yellow bisque with light blue urn applied to the disk; self-shank; made for the yearly meeting of the Wedgwood seminars held in the United States; 1 in/2.5 cm.
2. Oval mounted in silver, c 1880, ⅝ in/1.6 cm. Metal shank molded in the silver mounting.
3. Cupid in gold-washed mounting, c 1985. Made for Jessie Partt for button collectors; ½ in/1.3 cm. 1 in/2.5 cm cut also available.
4. Eighteenth century disk with conventional design set in Boulton steel mounting with cut steel trim in the center. 1½ in/3.8 cm with shank molded from steel mounting.

EIGHTEENTH-CENTURY
.... CERAMIC BUTTONS ....

The Meissen factories were started, and soon, French factories, especially Sèvres, adopted this type of ceramic ware, and factories opened in Staffordshire in England. Eighteenth-century ceramic buttons are scarce today. Some collectors have found buttons with backmarks of the famous factories – the crossed swords of Meissen or the crossed L's of Sèvres. These backmarks are believed to be fakes, so collectors need to beware. Buttons do not seem to have been important in the early ceramic factories of Europe.

Collectors, however, do find the stoneware or jasperware of Josiah Wedgwood mounted in copper or steel frames. He created small plaques which were glazed with a matt rather than a shiny finish, and the characteristic white bisque design overlay was placed on a plain, usually blue or black, background. Wedgwood, unlike the other companies, was very involved in button production, since the small metal frames were perfect holders for his creations. Mounted in metal after 1768 and with self-shanks after 1786, these buttons were so popular that they were copied by other potters, and their importance is evident since collectors strive to have at least one. Their rarity, desirability, age, and artistry make Wedgwood buttons very expensive.

BELOW
Sets of monochrome transfers on white disks mounted in brass frames were made in Paris in the 1870s, but are called "Liverpool Transfers" by collectors, after the city where Sadler and Green invented the technique at the beginning of the nineteenth century.

1.,5. Two of a set of eight, twelve, or sixteen buttons showing Zeus and Aphrodite. Mounted in brass with Paris backmarks, and a loop shank; 1¼ in/3.2 cm.
2. Same style as 1.,5.; ½ in/1.3 cm.
3. Egyptian head, one of matching pairs which face each other; Paris backmark; 1¼ in/3.2 cm.
4 One of a set of French kings, with Paris backmark; 1½ in/3.8 cm, mounted in brass.

NINETEENTH-CENTURY
········· CERAMIC BUTTONS ·········

Ceramic buttons of the nineteenth century, with a variety of decorations to enhance the plain glazed finish, are more easily available to collectors. Buttons decorated with transfers occur in both monochrome and polychrome designs. A picture printed on paper was transferred to the button and re-fired in the kiln so that the design became glasslike and adhered. In 1757 Sadler and Green of Liverpool, England, developed the use of transfer decals on tiles, and the process was widely adopted by manufacturers throughout Europe. Most of these buttons were made in France from about 1860 and had nothing to do with Sadler and Green, their company, or Liverpool, so the general name "Liverpool Transfers," used for these buttons, can be misleading to a new collector.

ABOVE
Polychrome transfers of classical heads and Greek gods were embellished with hand painting, using gold to highlight the design, and were probably made in Paris in the 1870s.

1.,3.,4.,5. Four of a set of eight or twelve showing the Greek gods and demi-gods; mounted in brass; 1 in/2.5 cm; tin back.
2. Small ½ in/1.3 cm, probably one of set of twelve or sixteen of classical heads; brass mounting.

Often Liverpool Transfers are mounted in metal, and classical heads, birds, and flowers are the dominant pictorials. Monochromes of black, sepia, gold, or red are found in buttons of all sizes. Sometimes, the transfers were enhanced with hand painting. These additional colors, particularly the use of gold, either on the design or in the background, makes the button appear to be entirely hand-painted. With the development of lithography, the use of polychrome transfers on buttons increased.

In 1840 Richard Prosser of Birmingham patented a process in which a die was used to form plaster of Paris molds into which very fine powder resembling crushed porcelain rather than moist clay was pressed. After the powdered clay was removed from the form, a gradual build-up of many layers of white or colored slip, a semi-liquid water and clay mixture resembling paint, was added to the surface design so that shading was created in the recesses of the molding. Then the button was fired to create a shiny finish. Prosser sold this patent for his process, which allowed an increased rate of production since the buttons did not have to be formed by hand before they were decorated, to the Minton Company of Stoke-on-Trent in 1844, and the company became very involved in the production of ceramic buttons. Collectors call decoration by this method "pâte-sur-pâte," and a ceramic collection should include this type of button.

Besides handpainted, transfer, and pâte-sur-pâte techniques, other methods of decoration were achieved. Gilding, an application of honey gold or mercuric gold, was used by English potters mimicking the application of gold leaf by the Chinese. Honey gold was a combination of gold leaf and honey, which was affixed to the button and fired at a low temperature. In mercuric gilding a mixture of mercury and gold was applied to the porcelain, and when the button was fired at a low temperature, the mercury evaporated. Ceramicists also used silvered overlay to decorate ceramic buttons.

Potters also experimented with decorative glazes. In 1898 W Howson Taylor, a British art potter influenced by the Arts and Crafts movement of the late nineteenth century, by the Chinese porcelains of the Ming dynasty, and by the art critic John Ruskin, established the Ruskin Art Pottery in

ABOVE
In the 1830s, Minton and Company developed the pâte-sur-pâte technique in which slip is layed on a button to create shadowing in the depth of the color. This can be seen on the waves on this small, ½ in/1.3 cm button with a self-shank. These buttons are rare since the technique was not popular in men's clothing.

ABOVE
Ceramic buttons of the mid-nineteenth century were decorated with gold and silver overlays to embellish center designs. These were glazed in earlier firings so that plain self-shank disks became elaborate creations of color and gilt or silver.

1.,2.,3.,5.,6. 1 in/2.5 cm buttons showing many firings, in which color and a design were fired. The gold was either a paste of honey and gold, or mercuric gold; self-shanks; c 1860, or later.
4. Small, ⅝ in/1.6 cm button with silver overlay wreath design around the edge to border the painting of a woman in an eighteenth century costume; self-shank.

ABOVE

As part of the Arts and Crafts movement in the late nineteenth century, the English potter W Howson Taylor opened the Ruskin pottery near Birmingham. Each button was back-marked with the incised "Ruskin" and fastened to fabric with large self-shanks.

1. Octagonal souffle glaze of various pastels.
2.,3.,4. Mottled glaze of the same shade with depth of color variation to imitate Sing and Ming vases.

Smethwick, England. He tried to emulate the Chinese glazes which were the only decoration on the button. In the first attempts, called "Souffle Wares," the button is decorated in varying shades of one color. At one end the glaze was a darker shade and became lighter and mottled as the eye moved to the other end. In "Lustre Wares," all the colors of the spectrum were used. Taylor was most proud of his "High-Fired Wares," which were the most experimental. These are mottled with beautiful vivid coloring – oatmeal brown and pale gray splashed with red. Collectors will find buttons with the first two types of glazing; "High-Firing" was used primarily on large pieces like vases and urns. Buttons after 1904 are backmarked "Ruskin," so they are easily identifiable. Works before 1904 used the initials "WHT" with a mark resembling a pair of scissors, but the mark is not found on buttons. The Ruskin Art Pottery remained in business and made buttons until 1935, but before he died, Taylor destroyed all his records and papers so that no one else could continue his factory.

ABOVE

Buttons made from streaked clays found near New England potteries in the early nineteenth century were rough-hewn and used as fasteners called Norwalk pottery by collectors.

1.,2.,3.,4. Small ½ in/1.3 cm vest or sleeve buttons mounted in brass with a flexible loop shank; variations in color from the color striations in the clay.
5.,7. Heavy pinshank buttons with loop shank formed from the centered pin; ¾ in/2 cm.
6. Metal escutcheon of woman's head in plain rounded clay disk with plate and loop shank; 1 in/2.5 cm.
8. Unusual four-hole sew-through; 1 in/2.5 cm.

Potters in the northeastern United States used a combination of different colored clays as the basis for their decoration, and the Norwalk-type button was produced. Before the second firing, a colorless glaze or one of blue, green, or yellow was applied. In the late eighteenth and early nineteenth century, stoneware factories in Bennington, Vermont, and Norwalk, Connecticut, produced coarse household goods which collectors associate with early Americana. These goods, usually mottled in shades of brown with other colors splattered or streaked into the design, were available throughout New England. Although company records of the Bennington works do not indicate that buttons were made there, records of the Connecticut companies show that buttons were a very important business from 1825 to 1853. While some early buttons were hand-formed, later ones seem to have been formed in a mold.

·FAR EASTERN CERAMIC BUTTONS·

European ceramics were based on those crafted in the Orient. The Chinese and the Koreans were the earliest potters, developing arts in the medium centuries before the process began in Europe. It is the Japanese, however, whose ceramics are treasured by button collectors as they gather Satsuma and Arita buttons. Satsuma buttons became available to the West with Matthew Perry's trade agreement with the Japanese in 1854. Japanese arts were popular in Paris and London in the 1870s, and merchants sold sets of Satsuma buttons to the Europeans; their popularity continued through the 1950s when the button industry was one of the important economic features of post-war Japan. Soldiers returning from their postings and early tourists brought home sets of Japanese buttons. The tradition of the ceramicists in the Satsuma region, however, can be traced back to the sixteenth century, when captured Korean potters were brought back to Japan by Shimaza Yoshiro, Lord of Satsuma. These skilled slaves began working in an earthenware process similar to faience later developed in France. Designs were hand painted in black on a fired white clay disk. Then, after each color was added, the button was fired at an appropriate temperature. Finally, stippling and painting in 24-karat gold was applied, and the button was polished with a glass brush. The Satsuma button is characterized by a cream background with a crackle finish handpainted with oriental motifs of flowers, birds, and traditionally clothed Japanese men and women. Twentieth-century buttons depict scenes, the Shinto mythology, and animals more appropriate to western settings. Some Satsumas are found with matt black or highly glazed cobalt blue backgrounds or borders. Sizes vary, but a button less than ⅜in/1cm in diameter is rare. Some of the buttons were set in a silvered metal base with loop shank, but most have self-shanks. Although Satsuma buttons are plentiful since they were so popular, they are much sought by collectors, and even modern ones have become expensive.

After World War II, potteries in the Arita area near Kyoto began to create buttons and jewelry plaques from the local porcelain materials. These buttons, molded and painted to a matt or polished finish, are often found as realistics, a molded

ABOVE

Satsuma buttons, characterized by their cream color and crackle glaze, were imported in sets of six into a European market which desired all things Japanese. The buttons became available to collectors after World War II.

1. Floral design of chrysanthemum and cherry blossoms with heavy gold stippling and black border. Marked with red circle enclosing a cross, the royal Satsuma mark; 1¼ in/3.2cm; c 1890.
2. Scene of seated Japanese musicians; self-shank; 1½ in/3.8 cm; c 1890.
3. Modern button of two geisha; less gold used, except as outline for the button; 1 in/2.5 cm, c 1950.
4. Unusual button of immortals and young men and boys with heavy gilding and royal backmark; self-shank; 1 in/2.5 cm; c 1880.
5. Scene of Mount Fuji and lake below, mounted in silver; ⅝ in/1.6 cm; c 1930.
6. Octagonal scene of Mount Fuji with black dotted border; self-shank; ½ in/1.3 cm; c 1920.
7. Geisha in pentagon shape with scalloped border; self-shank; ¾ in/2 cm; c 1930.

form shaped like what is depicted. Other buttons are round or rectangular with birds, flowers, or the Seven Immortals in vivid colors applied to black backgrounds. Most are medium-sized, but some are very large, over 2in/5cm in length. Most have self-shanks, but large ones often have a double metal shank applied to the porcelain back. These buttons have become highly collectible and very expensive.

Many ceramic buttons can be viewed as miniature artworks, but one type was a utilitarian fastener even when it was introduced in the early nineteenth century – the common china button. Using the process developed by Prosser in England for molding buttons before they were decorated and fired, potters could use a variety of simple body shapes made in die-cast molds. Since detailed decoration was not needed, buttons could be glazed with basic colors and manufactured rapidly and inexpensively. The French, particularly JF Bapterosses, adopted this manufacturing method, and Thomas Prosser, Richard's brother, emigrated to the United States and took the method there also. The English companies were gradually forced from the market, and Minton had stopped making buttons by the mid-1850s.

····· COLLECTING CHINA BUTTONS ·····

By far the best place for the new collector to begin is with the calico. Cotton printed cloth manufactured in Calcutta, India, and exported to England was called calico. Collectors refer to china buttons printed with the design of the fabric as calicoes. These buttons were made by laying the transfer sheet over all

the buttons, and cutting away the unused section of transfers. Most of the bodies are white, but other body colors like blue, black, brown, green, and pink may be found, usually in the small size. Over 326 calico button designs have been recorded and classified. Often the designs are found in several colors, so the collector could make a life-time study of this type of button. While most calico buttons are four-hole sew-throughs with a raised rim, collectors look for other body types like a concave shape and a two-hole, elongated "fish-eye" sew-through. Several designs with medium pin-shanks have also been found. A small, domed plaque mounted in a metal frame called a calico jewel is also sought by collectors. The most desirable calico buttons are medium-sized and may be plain or rimmed.

The igloo, considered to be the rarest of all china buttons, has a unique construction. It has a base disk with two holes like an ordinary sew-through. A small dome is placed in the center over the two holes, and at its base are openings on each side through which the thread passes. Sewing this button onto a garment must have been difficult; perhaps this is why they are so scarce – they weren't functional. Other body types include the inkwell, the dish, the tire, the pie-crust rim, the sawtooth rim, and the hobnail and inverted hobnail rim. The whistle, a button with one hole on the face and two holes on the back, is another body type. There are many molds for whistle buttons from bumpy berry tops to domed ones.

Shoe buttons, smock buttons, gaiter buttons, and panty-waists describe the function of the china button. Bull's-eyes and ringers describe the use of circular painted designs on solid-colored, usually white, bodies. Inserted shanks, bird-cage shanks, and metal loop shanks are used as other classifying methods.

Gingham and stencils, like calico, refer to the designs on the face of the button. To make calico buttons, the design is applied only once. In ginghams, a two-step process is used. No design is repeated on a stencil button, and it is usually of a single color. The body is white or cream and plain in shape. Over 60 different designs have been cataloged, each available in many colors, providing another excellent way for a beginner to start a collection.

BELOW

From the mid-nineteenth century, buttonmakers made utilitarian fasteners from porcelain for everyday clothing for men and women.

1. Four-hole inverted hobnail border; 1 in/2.5 cm.
2. Brown tire-rim four-hole sew-through.
3. Bird-cage shank with fluted top and mottled center disk.
4. Scalloped rim, white china button; four-hole sew-through.
5. Hobnail and banded gaiter button; orange luster decorates the center.
6. Gingham china to match gingham fabric; four-hole sew-through.
7. Stencil china in lavender; two-hole sew-through.
8. Inkwell shape with four-hole sew-through; mottled brown and blue; ½ in/1.3 cm.
9. Inkwell banded in orange, gold, and green on white china; four-hole sew-through.

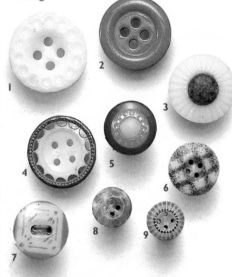

BELOW

Modern studio buttonmaker Lois Calkins created this nursery rhyme set of Humpty Dumpty, as well as other rhymes, for collectors in the 1950s, and they are still available from her today. Using transfer designs enhanced with hand-painting, white porcelain disks with self-shanks show the techniques used by potters in the eighteenth century.

ENAMEL BUTTONS

CHAPTER 6

For centuries craftsmen have prized enameling, and the technique has changed little since the sixteenth century. Colored, opaque or transparent glass is reduced to a fine powder and applied to a metal surface, usually gold, silver, brass, or copper. The glass is then melted and fuses to the metal by heat. Buttons decorated in this fashion, called "enamels," are highly prized.

Cloisonné is one of the oldest enameling techniques. Thin wires or bands of metal are bent into a design and soldered to a base to form an open-work pattern of spaces or partitions (*cloisons*). The spaces are filled with powdered enamel fused by heating. Because the enamel shrinks during firing, the process is repeated until the fused enamel is level with the wire. Counterenameling, or coating the back of the piece, may be used to ease the strain on the metal. Then the surface is polished smooth.

From its Byzantine origins until the early twentieth century, cloisonné was one of the rarest forms of enamel. Cloisonné buttons are scarce; most found today are from this century.

The technique of champlevé is opposite to cloisonné. Instead of building up the design, it is carved or stamped out of a single piece of metal. The hollows are filled with powdered enamel, and the object is fired. The metal base can be prepared by hand using engraving tools or by machine using a die to stamp the pattern into the metal base. A machine-stamped button can usually be distinguished by the pattern of the die visible on the back. Sometimes the champlevé technique was used for the border of a button.

Champlevé is simple and relatively inexpensive, and most nineteenth-century enamel buttons were produced by this technique. Champlevé buttons are the easiest enamels to acquire.

Basse-taille enameling, first done by Italian goldsmiths in the thirteenth-century, is a refinement of the champlevé technique. The stamped or engraved depressions have patterns of wavy lines in low relief which are filled with layers of translucent enamel to give a shaded effect. On some buttons the background pattern, covered by colored translucent enamel, is the only design of the button.

TOP RIGHT

The **Chinese** developed the fragile cloisonné enamel buttons shown in these two examples from *c* 1900, in which small cells, called *cloisons*, formed with gold wire are filled with enameling material.

1. Center butterfly design of red, white, and blue on black field; ½ in/2.5 cm; worn on dresses, and at the shoulders of Oriental jackets.
2. Floral design with red and dark blue flowers on light blue background; ¾ in/ 2 cm; *c* 1900; same purpose as 1.

CENTER RIGHT

In the mid-nineteenth century the **French** developed champlevé enameling in which a base metal is stamped and these sections filled with enamel.

1. Intricate conventional design of five colors to imitate cloisonné; 1 in/2.5 cm; *c* 1870.
2. Champlevé combined with painted enameling to create shading; ¾ in/2 cm.
3. Openwork to suggest Art Nouveau influence; cut steels used to accent design; 1¼ in/3.2 cm; *c* 1890–1910.
4. Called Charlotte Corday; champlevé center design with cut steel border; possibly used as jewelry on a costume; 1½ in/3.8 cm; *c* 1870.
5. Champlevé border with painted enamel center; *c* 1870.

BELOW RIGHT

Basse-taille enameling was made by stamping a design, usually a rippled or sunburst effect, on the base and enameling on the surface.

1. Water lilies; brass; one-piece with applied loop shank; 1 in/2.5 cm; *c* 1870; French.
2. Cornflowers over clear enamel; silver base with sunburst. Sometimes these are hallmarked silver or marked "Sterling" indicating British or American manufacture; ¾ in/2 cm; *c* 1900 or later; French.
3. Elaborate painting with many colors; 1 in/2.5 cm; *c* 1890; probably French.

This technique could, with some handwork, be used for mass production, and many basse-taille buttons were produced around the turn of the century. Pairs of basse-taille cuff buttons on silver linked by a chain made in the 1930s account for the frequency of small basse-taille buttons with conventional designs found today.

Japanese buttons produced by the basse-taille technique are called *gin bari*. They are among the most beautiful basse-taille buttons, but are rare and expensive.

Plique-à-jour is a technique similar to cloisonné, but without the metal backing or disk. Fused glass fills the open spaces of the metal wire design to create a delicate piece that resembles a stained glass window. Very few of these fragile buttons are found today, and the price reflects their scarcity.

RIGHT

The Japanese developed the *gin bari* technique as an imitation of basse-taille which had been developed in Europe in the nineteenth century. Buttons were imported from Japan in sets for use on silk and satin fashions or on Oriental-styled jackets and dusters.

1. Butterflies around centered floral design with two-color background; ¾ in/2 cm; *c* early twentieth century.
2. Enameled disk of branch with cherry blossoms mounted in brass frame with twisted border; 1¼ in/3.2 cm; *c* early twentieth century.
3. Design mounted in plain brass mounting with applied loop shank; ¾ in/2 cm; *c* early twentieth century.

LEFT

The rare plique-à-jour enameling, French, *c* 1890–1900, which is illustrated by this stylized flower and leaves with Arts and Crafts-styled pewter mounting, has been compared with the construction of stained glass. The liquid glass is dropped into the metal section much like the colored glass is fitted between lead strips. This 1 in/2.5 cm button was worn on jackets or as an accent button on a cape.

······· PAINTED ENAMEL BUTTONS·······

Near the end of the fifteenth century, craftsmen discovered that enamel would cling to metal without the binding cloisons or champlevé cells, and that one layer of enamel could be fused to another without causing the first to separate from the metal. Painted enamels (*émaux peints*) developed quickly and soon became the most popular type of enamel. It was made in Limoges in the sixteenth and seventeenth centuries and in France and England during the eighteenth and nineteenth centuries. The metal base is built up with repeated coats of ground opaque glass, usually white, cobalt blue, or black, each one fired and polished. Then brightly colored paint mixed with ground glass was used to paint objects and miniature scenes, with each color ideally fired separately. A final transparent layer of clear enamel seals in the colors and gives greater depth and brilliance.

RIGHT

Border of cut steel and pastes set off the painting on French pictorial enamels of the mid-nineteenth century.

1. **Oval of magentas on white background, called "Dainty Maid;" grain set paste border; applied loop shank; silvered brass base; 1¼ in/3.2 cm.**
2. **Pastel flowers on white background; oval; cut steel borders; brass base; applied loop shank; 1 in/2.5 cm.**
3. **Shepherdess in eighteenth-century costume in pastels with white background; cut steel border; applied loop shank; brass base; 1 in/2.5 cm.**

BELOW RIGHT

From the eighteenth century on foil was used to enhance enamel designs, creating intricate embellishments which were protected by a transparent enamel coat.

1. **Rooster crowing at the dawning sun; basse-taille on stamped design enhanced by foil; brass base; applied loop shank; 1½ in/3.8 cm; early twentieth century.**
2. **Modern French enamel, c 1930s; silver foil flowers on blue background protected with transparent enamel; mounted in brass frame; applied loop shank.**
3. **Elaborate early nineteenth century enamel disk with circle of foil paillons around center floral design; mounted in brass frame with paste border; applied loop shank.**

Perhaps the most famous enamel factory was at Battersea, in London, England, where Stephen Theodore Jansson and his associates applied transfer printing from paper over a fired base coat. Their factory failed within three years, but large quantities of painted and transfer-printed enamel trinkets and buttons were produced in the North of England during the last 30 years of the eighteenth century. Buttons from this period are easy to recognize as the enameling is done on a thin copper base.

Painted enamel buttons, most produced in France, again became fashionable during the latter part of the nineteenth century. The base material was usually brass, and steel, beadlike enamel dots to imitate jewels and known as encrusted enamel, and champlevé enamel were used for the borders. Some of these buttons display very fine hand painting, but some were probably transfer-printed and filled in by hand. The term "Limoges" is used to describe buttons with an overall coating of enamel. There is no evidence that they were actually made in Limoges, but they are French.

BELOW

Borders of cut steel, pastes, enamel pierreries, and stamped metal provide frames for enamel work in the center of the French nineteenth century buttons.

1. Floral design; brass base; stamped openwork flower board; applied loop shank; 1½ in/3.8 cm.
2. Paste border around painting of woman; brass base; applied loop shank; 1 in/2.5 cm.
3. Young man offering flowers to woman in matching button; center disk mounted in brass frame with elaborate rococo border of scroll, flowers, and foliage.
4. Nocturnal scene of mountain and castle; champlevé with cut steel border; applied loop shank; brass base; 1 in/2.5 cm.
5. Square with center painted design of flowers; border of turquoise enamel pierreries; brass base; applied loop shank.

By the end of the nineteenth century, the quality of painting had deteriorated. The Art Nouveau movement in the early twentieth century revived excellence in design and craftsmanship, and high-quality enamel buttons, often on silver with Art Nouveau designs, were made during this period. Painted enamels with floral and conventional designs are abundant and relatively inexpensive, whereas the finer painted enamels with scenes and figures are not as plentiful and have always been expensive.

"En grisaille" describes the sixteenth-century art of applying white enamel on a black enamel background to create a design in shades of gray. Coat after coat of black ground glass is fired onto the metal disk and polished to make the background. Then thick or thin layers of white enamel are added to make the design. To create the characteristic subtle shading, a sharp pointed instrument is used to hatch fine lines through the layer of white to the dark undercoat, creating a design in black and white only.

Although true enamel painting in grisaille has rarely been used on buttons, collectors call enamel buttons with white painting on a black background "grisaille." They are not as plentiful as other painted enamel buttons.

Some fine modern painted enamel buttons were made by Motiwala Brothers in Bombay, India, in the 1950s. Motiwala advertised hand-made buttons in the *National Button Bulletin*, and many collectors took advantage of his offer. Religious themes were the most popular and are the easiest to find. Other subjects include the coronation of Queen Elizabeth II and Kate Greenaway scenes. The company also made lovely basse-taille enamels.

·········· COLD ENAMEL BUTTONS ··········

The Germans are responsible for a cheap substitute for enamel, called "kalt" or "cold" enamel. Since true enamel must be fired, this is a contradictory term, used for various low-price substitutes for enamel in which the metal surfaces were colored with baked-on or low-fired material. Although the finish looks similar to real enamel, it flakes off easily with use. These buttons are attractive, and their price should reflect the fact that they are not true enamel.

ABOVE

Called "en grisaille," meaning "in shades of gray," this technique is characterized by the build-up of layers of white enamel on a black, dark gray, or dark blue surface so that the pictorial appears shaded. Few of these buttons exist although some people incorrectly call all black-and-white buttons by this name. Set in brass frame with applied loop shank; ½ in/1.3 cm; *c* early nineteenth century; French.

ABOVE

In the 1950s and 1960s the firm of Motiwala Brothers in Bombay, India, provided enameled picture buttons for collectors using a technique similar to that of using photographs as transfers. Collectors often sent pictures of what was to be shown on the face of the button and received 1¼ in/3.2 cm silver buttons with an enamel picture.

1. Scene from a Kate Greenaway drawing; since collectors were very interested in her illustrations, many sets were produced.
2. Santa Claus.
3. Jean Millet painting of "The Angelus" showing the use of many colors to imitate the painting.

-NATURAL- MATERIALS

No. 2127

CHA**7**TER

Early humans formed fasteners from the materials on hand. Bone, ivory, vegetable ivory, pearl and shell, and wood are natural materials from which buttons have been made since there have been buttons. Horn or hooves were sometimes used in their natural states, but usually they, like hard rubber, were processed. With minimal processing, all these substances can be carved, molded, painted, dyed, stenciled, or decorated with metal escutcheons, glass pastes, or other material inlays.

·················· I V O R Y A N D B O N E ··················

Ivory is the hard, white dentine which makes up the tusks of elephants, whales, hippos, and walruses. Since its sources are limited, it has always been considered a precious material, fine-grained and capable of taking a high polish density. Because of its denseness, it can be beautifully carved or used as a surface for paintings.

Collectors seek carved buttons from Asia, as well as modern Eskimo carvings which were made primarily for the twentieth-century tourist trade. Miniature paintings on ivory mounted under glass, which were made in the eighteenth century, are the most prized ivory buttons.

Manufacturers began to use animal bones to imitate expensive ivory buttons as early as the eighteenth century. After the bones were cleaned and boiled, disks were cut and turned to form medium-size buttons in which a pin shank was inserted. On a farm, where all parts of a slaughtered animal were used, itinerant button makers would produce these useful fasteners on the spot.

Bone is less dense than ivory and becomes brittle with age. When scraped with a knife, it comes off in a fine powder. Small black flecks often appear in the grain. Still, these simple buttons are highly collectible today. Small, sew-through buttons, made for utilitarian use such as underwear fasteners, are very common and available in two, three, four, and five-hole sew-throughs.

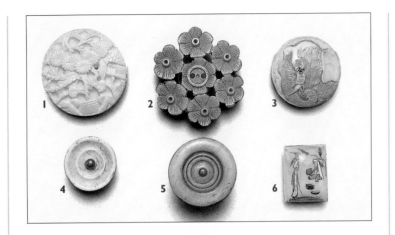

H A R D   R U B B E R

Hard rubber has been known since the mid-eighteenth century when explorers brought it from Brazil. However, it could not easily be used in button production, since processing was needed. Natives in Malay, however, did use gutta percha, a similar dark substance from a tree, to make knife handles, and by 1850 British, French, and American manufacturers used this substance for many things, including buttons.

An American, Charles Goodyear, became interested in using India rubber. Working with Nathaniel Hayward in 1839, Goodyear secured a patent for vulcanization, a process using extreme heat and sulfur with hard rubber to form products. On May 6, 1851, Nelson Goodyear perfected his brother's concept and was granted a patent on the button-making process. Two American companies, the Novelty Button Company and the India Rubber Comb Company, manufactured buttons until the patent expired in 1870. Then other companies manufactured buttons until the turn of the century.

These buttons are usually black or brown. Over 300 conventional designs are recorded, and these buttons are plentiful and inexpensive. Buttons with pictorial designs, manufactured in the late 1800s, are scarce.

LEFT
Carved bone and ivory have been used in buttons since the late eighteenth century.

1. Intricately carved ivory pot and plant; probably Japanese intended for export in sets; c 1920.
2. Design of flower heads in bone; probably Japanese intended for export in sets; 2 in/5 cm; c 1930.
3. Carved, tinted ivory elephant head; 1½ in/3.8 cm; early twentieth century.
4.,5. Ivory and bone pinshank buttons of late eighteenth and early nineteenth century; used for men's clothing on jacket and trousers; show design created by simple lathe turning; 1 in/2.5 cm.
6. Rectangular bone; painted desert oasis scene; c 1950; probably made in Middle East.

BELOW
The use of natural rubber and gutta percha for buttons in the mid-nineteenth century provided durable fasteners on which the designs were molded in dark brown or black colors.

1. Conventional design on rubber button; used on man's jacket or vest; metal shank; ⅝ in/1.6 cm.
2. Rubber button in dome shape with pinshank inserted through the button; same use as 1, ¾ in/2 cm.
3. Molded woman's head raised above a ¼ in/1.6 cm thick disk on rubber button; metal shank; 1 in/2.5 cm.
4. Anchor button made by US Rubber Company; originally for naval peacoats, later used in sailor fashions; design is pressed into the button; ½–2 in/3.8–5 cm.
5. Gutta percha button showing wheat; used as coat button; 2 in/5 cm; c 1870.

···············HORN···············

From earliest times, man has made fasteners from the horns and antlers of the animals around him. Usually these buttons, as well as the ones found into the mid-nineteenth century, used the bony interior of the horn, which was cut into disks and polished. Holes were drilled so that the button could be sewn onto a garment. These early buttons are difficult to find, and they may be ignored since they were utilitarian without much beauty. Peasants in Austria and Switzerland, however, carved horn buttons depicting local animals and flowers, they are available and popular.

In the early 1800s a "plastic" horn button appeared. Boiling the horns and hooves of cattle, sheep, buffalo, or deer made them soft and pliable. This substance could be made into a semi-solid mixture which button makers could cut into blanks. These pieces were laid in molds, and metal shanks were inserted. Clamps were applied to form the button, which was prized out of the mold with a sharp metal pick, leaving a small identifying hole on the back of the button and giving them their name of pick buttons.

While early molded horn buttons were of simple conventional designs, later ones, many with a Paris backmark, were pressed into molds using a hydraulic press which allowed more beautiful pictorials. Some were dyed golden tan or red, but most horn buttons are black, making the design difficult to see without careful study, but their beauty and their rarity make them highly collectible. Unfortunately, horn deteriorates and is susceptible to small mites. To preserve the buttons, collectors need to examine them carefully and brush and clean them frequently to prevent destruction.

BELOW

Horn buttons, made from the processing of hooves and horns of cattle and horses, were molded into simple dark fasteners in the 1870s and later. They were picked out of the molds, leaving the characteristic "pick mark" on the back which helps collectors identify them.

1.,2.,3.,5. Heads of women often found on these buttons.
4. Head of Queen Elizabeth II, probably from the coronation; silvered with thin coat of paint to simulate a metal button.

LEFT

Manufacturers, probably in France, of the mid-nineteenth century, created beautiful buttons with horn bases using gold, silver, and pearl.

1. Tan base to suggest tortoise shell; silver rose highlighted with gold and pearl flecks; metal shank; 1 ¼ in/3.2 cm.
2. Opaque horn base with inlay of silver dragon; metal shank; 1 ½ in/3.8 cm.
3. Translucent red horn with pearl and silver with a center flower of pearl; metal shank; 1 ¼ in/3.2 cm.
4. Cupid of silver inlaid in dark horn base; ⅝ in/1.6 cm.
5. Rectangular shape of translucent tan horn base with inlay of silver and pearl to create floral design; metal inserted shank; ¾ in/2 cm long.
6. Basket of flowers of dyed pearl inlay in opaque horn base; ⅝ in/1.6 cm.
7. Violet of dyed mother-of-pearl in opaque horn base; ⅝ in/1.6 cm.

ABOVE

Deluxe carved pearl buttons, probably completed by Italian masters from 1860 to the early 1900s, were made from the shells of pearls and oysters since the layers of color from brown to gray to white provided variations which the artists incorporated into their works.

1. Center design of the Taj Mahal; 1½ in/3.8 cm.

2. Brown carving on intricately carved background of white pearl; applied cut steels possibly needed to secure two-piece construction; heavy metal shank; 2 in/5 cm.

3. Carved house and woman mounted in steel frame with cut steel border; popular scene repeated in other sizes and other types of shell; 1 in/2.5 cm.

4. Center design of feeding stag of white pearl with gray border of leaves and corn; 1½ in/3.8 cm.

5. Plain white pearl background; applied cut steels; 2 in/5 cm.

Horn inlay buttons were blanks decorated by inlaying or impressing another material into the face of the button. Silver, pearl, brass, abalone, and bone were common materials used to create pictorial, geometric, or conventional designs. While horn was often the base material in inlays, other substances were also used: tortoise shell prepared as horn, glass, pearl, bone, and ivory are all found as the base of an inlay button. Inlays are highly collectible, and the pictorials, especially large ones with the pictures in precious metals, are very expensive indeed.

PEARL AND SHELL

The artistry and hand workmanship of pearl and shell buttons combine with their sheen and coloring to create some of the best buttons ever made.

Pearl buttons, with the iridescence which differentiates them from shell buttons, begin as blanks cut from the lining of the shell of a sea creature such as a mollusk or a sea snail. Plain pearl buttons, often called mother-of-pearl, with two or four-hole sew-throughs, are plentiful and inexpensive. The shading, size, or turned design on these plain buttons are what make them collectible. All white might be shaded to brown in Tahiti pearls; smoky pearls in shades of gray are also beautiful. Abalone, with its swirls of colors, is also popular, either by itself or combined with other pearls or shells. Large plain buttons, particularly ones with turnings to form a design, are desirable, but collectors avoid small and medium plain white pearl buttons even if they are old.

The most collectible pearl buttons were made in the eighteenth and nineteenth century, almost entirely by hand. Button blanks, cut from the washed animal shell, were engraved or carved and then polished by master craftsmen. The backs were often left unfinished; collectors can therefore see the natural state of the pearl and identify the animal used. Sometimes a shank was inserted into the back of the pearl or a pinshank put through the button, but often the finished plaque was mounted in a metal frame, decorated with pastes, or dyed to bring out the carving. While cameo or raised designs are popular, all types of carving, including intaglio in which the design is carved down into the pearl, and incising, in which a

Plain white pearl buttons were combined with other materials as trim to create deluxe buttons in the late nineteenth century.

1. Four-hole white pearl with conventional design of carved lines combined with turquoise enamel pierreries; 1¼ in/3.2 cm.
2. Plain white disk with center of mosaic inlaid black glass; heavy metal shank; 1½ in/3.8 cm.
3. "Liverpool Transfer" on white ceramic disk fitted in plain white pearl border; heavy metal shank; 1 in/2.5 cm.
4. White carved pearl openwork base with enameled openwork and glass paste trim to give three-material button; metal shank; 1 in/2.5 cm.
5. Paisley transfer; ½ in/1.3 cm.
6. Encrusted pictorial; ½ in/1.3 cm.
7. Dyed blue decorated with silver and gold foil to create floral design; rococo shape; metal shank; 1¼ in/3.2 cm.
8. Vest button with lithograph in center of a hunting scene; ½ in/1.3 cm with elongated vest shank.

design is created with a shallow line sometimes filled with paint, are found. Some pearl buttons were gilded or overlaid with silver as porcelain buttons were. Some buttons were decorated with metal escutcheons inserted by hand, popular in picture buttons. Even in the age of mass production, desirable pearl buttons required handwork using the same techniques as jewelry.

Freshwater pearl buttons have less iridescence than ocean pearls. By the late 1890s American button makers were manufacturing buttons from clam shells found in the upper Mississippi River valley, Connecticut, Maryland, Pennsylvania, and New England. These buttons do not have the jewelry-like workmanship of the European-made ocean pearl buttons. They were utilitarian, and the most collectible are mounted in metal with delicate metalwork over the face of the button.

Shell buttons are not iridescent. A variety of shells were used: cowrie, a mottled brown and white with a lavender undertint; helmet shell banded with layers of white or orange, tan, or rosy beige; pink queen conch; brown-spotted tiger cowrie with its porcelain-like finish. Pinna, a brown brittle

shell, is highly desirable. Carvers highlighted their cameo work with the colors, creating beautiful backgrounds for their skill.

VEGETABLE IVORY

In 1859 Johann Hille, an Austrian wood carver, is said to have presented to the European market carved and dyed buttons made from the corozo nuts of the tagua palm, which grows in the rainforests of Central and South America. The buttons resembled ivory, so the material was called *vegetable ivory* by the button trade. British manufacturers began production in the late 1850s and presented the buttons at the 1862 Universal Exposition in Paris. Factories were established in Leeds, Massachusetts, in 1860 and in Springfield, Massachusetts, in 1863 to mass-produce these small buttons. The French began making these buttons in the 1870s. Production declined after 1920, and by the 1940s few buttons were being made of vegetable ivory.

The nuts were dried and sliced into sheets from which blanks were cut. Only a few blanks could be cut from each slice, and large buttons are rare. The blanks were dyed, usually in dark colors like brown or red with lighter decoration added. Many were carved in delicate conventional designs, and others were stenciled in plaid patterns. A few pictorials, especially scenes, were dyed into the buttons. Many of the plain dye blanks were decorated with pierced or scrolled brass escutcheons of animals, flowers, people, or other objects.

BELOW

The most collectible vegetable ivory buttons are those decorated and combined with other materials.

1. Painted country scene; 1 in/2.5 cm; probably c 1940, Central America.
2. Metal embellishment with cut steel on a pinshank through a carved disk; 1 in/2.5 cm; c 1900.
3. Transfer of house with moon on smooth button; ⅝ in/1.6 cm.
4. Red dyed concave disk with raspberries in metal; applied metal shank; 1 in/2.5 cm.
5. Vegetable ivory frame with fabric background for metal shamrock; metal shank; ⅝ in/1.6 cm.
6. Embossed brown button of child in Greenaway-like costume; self-shank; ½ in/1.3 cm.
7. Scalloped disk, slight concave; self-shank.

Some interesting examples have designs incised into the dyed blank so that the natural off-white color showed. Sets of natural-colored blanks with handpainted scenes of Central American life are also found. Most of the buttons have self-shanks; a few have metal inserted shanks.

Today, B Blumenthal and Company is producing new vegetable ivory buttons. The plain, utilitarian modern buttons, dyed with non-toxic, non-polluting dyes, are produced under the LaMode label. Carded and displayed as Tagua Nut Buttons from the Rainforest, they carry a notice to explain that Conservation International has begun a Tagua Initiative to support rainforest conservation and community development to provide jobs so that further clearing can be prevented.

Vegetable ivory buttons are plentiful and inexpensive, and they are sometimes overlooked by collectors. Beginners may find them an excellent way to study nineteenth-century manufacturing since a variety of techniques were used.

BELOW

Picture buttons of the late nineteenth century incorporated the use of wood, but the medium was not popular, and interesting wooden buttons of the period are rare.

1. Wooden disk with applied stamped brass showing heads of Jupiter and Minerva; metal shank; 1¼ in/3.2 cm.
2.,4. Wood used as the background of a pictorial button; thin sheet fitted behind the design; c 1880.
3. Brass rabbit and leaf on thick rough square of wood which is polished on the back; heavy metal shank; 2 in/5 cm.
5. Stamped design of a dog's head in leaves; plate and loop shank; Paris backmark; 1½ in/3.8 cm.

WOOD

In 1771, simple wooden buttons were advertised by Benjamin Randolph, a Philadelphia cabinet maker. Most were plain, thick disks with pin shanks or inserted bone shanks. Usually the wooden disks were used as molds over which fabric was drawn or embroidery completed. Sometimes the disks were painted. These are the eighteenth-century buttons which collectors seek.

In the mid-to-late nineteenth century, picture buttons were very popular, and Victorian manufacturers found that thin sheets of wood could be stamped just like metal sheets. Other wooden buttons were made by applying metal escutcheons with picture button designs onto wooden disks. Turned wood buttons were formed the way cabinet manufacturers made the

1   2   3   4

ornate furniture found in Victorian parlors. Picture buttons mounted on a background of thin wood are not classified as wooden buttons, but they are popular with collectors and show another use of wood in the nineteenth century.

In the twentieth century, wooden buttons were made by manufacturers and studio button makers. In the 1930s and 1940s, companies producing paper in Michigan and upper New York State combined excess wood pulp with glue to form "plastic wooden" buttons known as Burwood or Syroco. The semi-solid wood and glue paste was extruded and forced into molds, often the same designs used in making celluloid buttons of the period. These medium and large buttons, usually in brown or other dark colors, carry designs associated with football and other sports, war machines like tanks and airplanes, and castles and knights. Sometimes these buttons are painted in blue, green, or gold. More unusual designs show the Statue of Liberty, floral designs, and animals.

During World War II and into the 1950s, when metals were scarce, wooden buttons were made in various shapes, combined with Bakelite and other plastics, and decorated with transfers, paint, and trims. Charming children's buttons showing pictorials were popular during this time. Studio button makers, who make buttons for collectors rather than for use, have used wood in marquetry, inlays, and carvings.

In addition to the natural materials described, collectors will find buttons in coal, gemstones, lava, leather, tortoise shell, and coral, and even straw has been fashioned into woven buttons. A button maker is limited only in his or her artistry in making a fastener.

ABOVE
Burwood and Syroco buttons of the 1920–1940 period were the first "plastic" wooden buttons, since a mixture of wood and a glue substance was extruded and molded into large buttons; usually associated with boys' clothing.

1. Oval football quarterback; two-hole sew-through; traditional brown finish.
2. Openwork showing pre-Civil War Southern mansion and carriage; detail of design is significant; 2 in/5 cm.
3. Openwork of a bird on a bough.
4. Castle with knights in the foreground; stained brown; 2 in/5 cm.

BELOW
Wood became a popular medium in modern buttons of the 1940s–1960s.

1. Carved and painted convex disk to create mask effect by contrast of blue and light wood; c 1960.
2. Painted floral bouquet; bark around the edges; c 1945.
3. Painted wooden disk with bear character in a sailor's outfit; c 1980.
4. Studio button of Tim Dippold using inlay of wood (marquetry) to create the design; c 1985.
5. Stamped and painted wooden design of young girl in Tyrolean costume; ⅝ in/1.6 cm; c 1950.
6. Realistic guitar; painted and lacquered with metal shank; c 1955.

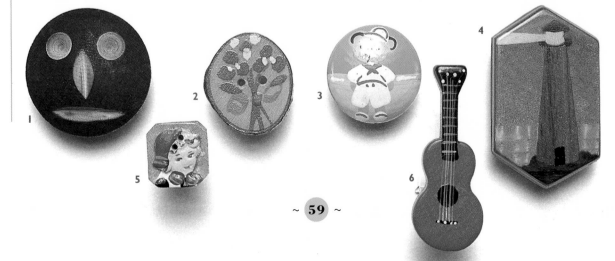

Plastic Buttons

For some, "plastic" conjures up an image of useful modern items such as kitchen containers or children's toys. When "antique plastic" is mentioned, it seems to be a contradiction. In fact, plastics in synthetic form such as celluloid have been around for more than 100 years and in natural form, such as horn, for much longer.

The word "plastic," which comes from the Greek word, *plasticos*, meaning able to retain any shape into which it is molded, came into common usage in the 1920s. There are two types of plastic materials: thermoplastic and thermosetting. Thermoplastic substances, such as celluloid, can be reheated and reformed. Thermosetting substances can be molded when heated, but the reaction is accompanied by a chemical change, so the material is permanently hardened and heat-resistant thereafter. Examples are Bakelite and casein.

Plastics can also be classified as natural, semisynthetic, and synthetic. Natural plastics are found in nature and include horn, gutta percha, lacquer, and amber. Semisynthetic plastics, made by modifying the chemical composition of a natural material, include casein and celluloid. Synthetic plastics are entirely man-made and include acrylic (trade names Lucite and Plexiglas) and Bakelite.

During the late nineteenth century, the button industry began to use new synthetic plastics that allowed unheard of versatility in color and design in mass-manufactured buttons. However, the earlier plastics also had shortcomings. Substances released as the plastic slowly decomposes cause metal on the button to corrode, and other metal buttons stored with early plastic buttons will also corrode.

CELLULOID

Celluloid was the first semisynthetic plastic. In 1870, an American printer, John Wesley Hyatt, patented a formula for his attempt to find a substitute for ivory billiard balls, a mixture of nitrocellulose and camphor. Although his plastic proved to be too brittle for its intended purpose, it was used for many other household items, and by the end of the century Hyatt's trade name, "Celluloid," was part of the language.

Celluloid was first used on buttons as a substitute for glass. Because it could also be made to imitate ivory, coral, jade, marble, glass, wood, and horn and was available in 200 different colors, it was soon used as a structural material for buttons as well. Its popularity for buttons was at its height from the 1870s to the 1930s, although many buttons from the World War II era were also made of celluloid. Celluloid was also used as a trim or background material on metal buttons.

Some other terms used for types of celluloid buttons are "ivorine," "ivoroid," and "pyralin." Ivorine, originally a manufacturer's trade name, is used to describe celluloid that imitates ivory. Ivoroid is the term for a thin sheet of celluloid stamped with a design, tinted with color, and set in a metal back with a shank. Pyralin, DuPont's trade name, describes smooth ivory-colored celluloid with a pronounced grain.

To make sure a button is celluloid, some experts stick a hot needle – carefully – in an inconspicuous spot, which releases a faint smell of camphor. Others claim that the heat of the hand will release the characteristic odor.

Celluloid is very flammable, and as modern nonflammable plastics were developed, production of celluloid buttons ceased. Celluloid buttons are very popular with collectors, and many good examples of celluloid imitating other materials and used as a trim on metal buttons are available, but they have become expensive. Most are found in ivory or shades of brown. Ivoroid buttons are the hardest to find because they did not wear well, and pictorials are scarce and expensive.

ABOVE

Celluloid, available in buttons since the mid-nineteenth century, was used in a variety of forms, making it a valuable material into the twentieth century.

1. Called a "One-Piece Thirties;" modified square showing Art Deco influence; molded celluloid; used on women's coats; 2 in/5 cm; c 1930.
2. Classical head mounted in brass frame to imitate ivory; 1 in/2.5 cm; c 1920.
3. Imitation fabric with molding and color like silk moire; 1 1/4 in/3.2 cm; c 1920.
4. Tinted celluloid disk over foil mounted in brass frame to imitate basse-taille enamel; 1 in/2.5 cm; c 1920–30.
5.,7. Earliest use of celluloid as protective cover over lithograph; 7: use of celluloid in the border to imitate enamel pierreries; c 1890.
6. Celluloid in the center to imitate molded fabric; 3/4 in/2 cm; c 1900.

LEFT

In the late nineteenth century, celluloid provided a trim and background for metal buttons which were composed of up to 10 parts, all fitted into a japanned back with a loop shank. Used for women's coats and jackets, dark colors and shades of tan were often embellished with glass jewels.

TOP LEFT
Thin, stamped and tinted sheets of celluloid were fitted into brass frames to produce buttons called ivoroids, since they resembled carved ivory pictures.

1. Called "Lucy and Edgar," from the novel *The Bride of Lammermoor* by Sir Walter Scott; ¾ in/2 cm; c 1890.
2. Ivoroid sheet tinted brown with escutcheon of knight's helmeted head mounted in brass frame; 1 in/2.5 cm; c 1890.
3. Cupid with an umbrella in plain brass mounting; grained appearance to imitate ivory; 2 in/5 cm; c 1890.
4. Called "Flora and the Hind" or "Red Riding Hood;" celluloid over dark metal background; 1 in/2.5 cm.
5. Called "Christmas Angel;" ivoroid sheet is crimped over the metal back; 1 in/2.5 cm; c 1890.

CENTER LEFT
In the 1930s the Art Deco movement influenced the design of black and white/cream in the manufacture of buttons used for women's dresses, coats, jackets, and blouses, so that elaborate-appearing designs could be made inexpensively.

RIGHT
The first synthetic material, Bakelite, was used in the late nineteenth century as buttons and buckles were manufactured in dark colors.

1. Unusual Bakelite base decorated with an enamel disk; probably used on cloaks or coats; 2 in/5 cm; c 1890.
2. Brass Gibson head mounted on the Bakelite base; 2 in/5 cm; c 1890.
3. Elaborate leaf design in carved Bakelite.
4. Plain coat button with interesting shape.

ABOVE
Bakelite buttons of the 1940s emphasized realistic shapes and bright colors in their use on women's and children's everyday clothing.

1. Yellow flower pot; thin stamped sheet of Bakelite; sew-through.
2. Red pear in molded design; sew-through.
3. Heavy molded and carved tennis racquet; sew-through.
4. Heavy ocean liner in two colors with metal shank.
5. Blue elephant with metal tusk; metal shank.
6. Called "Krystel" Bakelite in crown with plastic jewels applied; painted to highlight design; c 1952, for coronation perhaps.

BAKELITE

Bakelite was the first entirely man-made plastic, and its manufacture signaled the beginning of the modern plastic industry. In 1907, Leo Baekeland took out his first patent related to the discovery of Bakelite. Originally the brand name of a phenolic compound, Bakelite has become a generic term as well.

By the early 1930s, Bakelite had almost completely replaced other plastics in the production of buttons. It was durable and could be molded, sliced, ground, or carved into many shapes. It was produced in a range of vibrant and nonfading colors, but because its resin was amber, it could not be made in white or pastel colors. Not many amber buttons are found; most are brown or black. Metal, paste jewels, and glass were all used as decoration on Bakelite buttons.

ABOVE
Lucite was important in buttons in 1950–60 as a plastic which could withstand washing machine treatment.

1.,4.,5. Carved back with painted design which shows through the lucite; metal shank.
2. Color added to make stripes in the material; square; metal shank.
3. Pearlized lucite flute and bead added to clear base; metal shank.

BELOW
Sets of six realistic buttons with the same theme, called "goofies" by collectors, were sold in fabric stores in the 1940s for use on home-sewn women's and children's clothing.

Top set: Teenage set.
Bottom set: 1939 World's Fair set.

Brightly colored novelty buttons made of Bakelite, called "realistics" by collectors, were shaped like the objects they were meant to represent. The Catalin Corporation used a similar material in the 1930s to produce a line of realistic fruits and vegetables in over 200 colors, which were among the most popular buttons of the period. Items made of Bakelite, including buttons, have become popular, but may be somewhat scarce and expensive.

CASEIN

Casein, another button plastic popular during the 1920s, '30s, and '40s, is still used today. Made from milk powder and chemicals, casein is white in its raw state. Early buttons were surface dyed and tended to fade with age. Because casein takes a high polish, it is also popular for buckles. Some early examples were marked "casein" on the back.

LUCITE

Acrylic, a lightweight, petrochemical plastic, appeared in the mid-1930s with the trade name "Lucite." Because of its translucence, it is used as a substitute for glass. A very versatile material, it can be molded, sawed, drilled, polished, and cemented to wood, metal, or plastic, and to itself. Many lucite buttons have carving and painting on the reverse side that shows through the clear plastic. Floral and conventional, nonpictorial motifs are most commonly found; rarer are bird designs and lucite trimmed with metal or paste jewels. Most lucite buttons are still inexpensive and readily available to collectors.

REALISTICS

A discussion on plastic buttons must mention realistic buttons, those which have the shape of the objects they represent. Most have an irregular outline, but a few have a geometric outer shape. For example, clock faces, coins, hats, and dinner plates are round; playing cards and dominoes are rectangular; pennants are triangular. In a 1942 button journal, Dorothy Foster Brown coined the term "goofies" for these odd or humorous designs, but most collectors now prefer to call these buttons "realistics."

Realistically shaped buttons became popular in the 1930s and '40s with the advent of the cheap plastic button. An endless variety of objects appeared, from animals to apparel to alphabets to flowers to fruits and vegetables to miniature reproductions of a steak dinner on a plate or cigarette boxes. The possibilities were endless, limited only by the imagination of the designer.

Although some were sold singly, realistics were often presented in sets, for example, six different garden implements, six buttons representing the 1939 World's Fair, or four of the same design. Cards with the title "Prevue Movie Buttons," featuring such stars as Jane Wyatt and Rudee Valee, were made. The same sets of buttons were often produced in many colors. They were fond in all chain and department stores and ranged in price from eight buttons for ten cents to over a dollar apiece. At first they were small – ½in/1.3cm to ¾in/2cm – but were later made in larger sizes. Realistics are fun to collect and often arouse the most admiration and comment from noncollectors.

A few realistic buttons are still being made today, but the sets and single realistic buttons from the 1930s and '40s are sought by collectors and are becoming scarce. A real find is a set on its original card.

Modern plastics changed the button industry. Plastic buttons are resistant to washing and heat, will not fade, and can be made to imitate almost any natural substance. Being machine-made, they do not display the craftsmanship and individual attention shown on buttons of earlier eras, but many fine examples of the variety of plastic buttons described here can be found.

UNIFORM BUTTONS

REG. Nº 7195 ↑

CHAPTER 9

There are as many different reasons to collect uniform buttons as there are collectors: as memorabilia from a given era, country, or industry; as mute witnesses to changes in government or the rise and fall of an industry, or evidence of socio-economic change. Others collect all buttons worn in a locality – by personnel of the government bodies such as police and fire departments, transportation companies, local industries, and schools, both private and public.

Like the uniforms to which they were once attached, uniform buttons were used to identify the wearer's unit, organization, or employer; to impress, or even to intimidate. A uniform button usually has a face design which is unique to the organization for which the button was made and was designed to be attached to the uniform permanently or semi-permanently. Permanent constructions have loops or "tunnels" on the back for sewing the button to the garment. Semi-permanent buttons have loop shanks which fit through a bound button hole and were fastened beneath the cloth with a triangle of leather or a metal toggle; they are not sewn on, but are worn like tuxedo studs. Top quality uniforms, particularly those likely to need frequent dry-cleaning, often had a placket, like an old-fashioned pants fly, in which the attachment was made. This inner lining prevented the shank and toggle from wearing out the cloth as it rubbed.

Collectors may find some buttons with shanks and other examples with identical designs that have wire prongs or threaded shanks, that were intended for use on hats or caps from which the buttons were not likely to be removed. True uniform buttons were not riveted to a garment, unlike many kinds of overall buttons.

················ METAL BUTTONS ················

Uniform buttons made from wood are very rare and usually appeared only during wartime in countries short on other materials. Metal buttons prior to the early 1830s were either a thick one-piece casting or brass stamping, or a thin stamping applied over wood or bone with the sew-on mechanism on the back. The castings were of gold or silver for officers and lead or pewter for enlisted men, and the shanks for attaching these buttons were cast into the button as it was made. The button

All the buttons on this page and on the next are brass, 1 in/2.5 cm and from the United States.

1. General Service, Army, 1854–1870.
2. General Service, Army, 1870–1902.
3. Infantry Officer, Army, 1855–1870.
4. General Service, Army, 1902–c1930.
5. US Marine Corps, enlisted, c 1870.
6. US Marine Corps, enlisted, c 1960.
7. Women's Army Auxiliary Corps, plastic, 1943–44.
8. Navy, pre-1942.
9. Navy, post-1942.
10. US Naval Reserve, World War II.
11. Air Force, present use.
12. US Lighthouse Service.
13. Customs Service.
14. US Prison Service.

material was often virtually the same as the bullets used in their weapons, so many soldiers in this period carried wooden or brass molds in which they could cast new bullets or buttons, or both, even melting their buttons into bullets if they ran out of lead. The official logo and membership button of the National Button Society carries the image of such a button mold.

With the Industrial Revolution, muscle power was replaced by water or steam power. Harder brass could be stamped into buttons, so the one-piece buttons became thicker and were made of brass plated with gold or silver. The more powerful stamping machines could imprint the front and the back of a button block at the same time, so a maker's or vendor's name could be marked on the reverse side as the design was impressed on the front. The attachment shank was most often soldered to the middle of the back in a separate operation, but a few buttons have been found with shanks formed in the initial stamping and the sewing eyes drilled through the shank later.

In the 1800s two patents revolutionized the manufacture of uniform buttons. The first of Benjamin Sanders' patents in England in 1813 permitted the use of very thin front and back pieces with the front piece turned over the edge of the back to which a shank had previously been attached. In the United States in 1832 "staff" construction meant that both the front and back were stamped from very thin pieces of brass. They were attached to one another by a ring of brass bent over the edges to form the buttons. In both types of button, the finished color was applied by plating or dipping either as the individual parts were made or when the button was completed, and both

15. **Fire Department, Rhode Island.**
16. **Police Department, Bristol.**
17. **Police Department, Philadelphia.**
18. **Park Police, Chicago, Illinois.**
19. **Grand Army of the Republic, staff type (uniform of veteran of US Civil War), 1870–1910.**
20. **American Legion, enameled, Veteran's Society, c 1910.**
21. **State Seal of Ohio.**

allowed a maker's or vendor's name and address to be stamped on the back of the button.

The finish even on good-quality metal buttons deteriorated from constant exposure to weather or usage, and many organizations used buttons of hot-stamped horn which were dyed black or sometimes red and had a brass loop shank inserted into the back. This construction was popular particularly in Great Britain well into the twentieth century. When Goodyear patented hard rubber, American button manufacturers quickly adopted it primarily for dress uniforms. Some fraternal organizations also used buttons of hard rubber.

In the 1890s, aluminum became cheap enough to roll into thin sheets, and a number of uniform button designs were made in both the Sanders and staff constructions, with aluminum as the face and back and brass as the shank material. The thin aluminum dented, and, contrary to original assumptions, it did lose its luster with use. It therefore fell out of favor, and few uniform buttons were stamped from sheet aluminum after World War I. However, aluminum die casting has returned to favor, and it is now the material of choice for all new uniform buttons throughout the British Commonwealth. These solid buttons can be plated, although many people object to the appearance of the finish, and they are found with a silver color or yellowish, off-gold color on military and transportation buttons.

The navies of the world wear white tropical uniforms which need very white buttons. Both glass and china could be molded with the required designs and were used until white plastic buttons gradually replaced them. The uniforms of many youth organizations such as Camp Fire Girls, Girl Scouts, and Boy Scouts also had glass buttons on shirts, blouses, dresses, and pants until these too were replaced by plastic.

Thermosetting plastic buttons first appeared in the late 1920s, often as a replacement for black horn. The plastic itself is often the desired color, black for Britain or blue/gray used by the Canadian railroad companies during World War II. If a conductive plastic material is used, the buttons can be plated like metal, a technique particularly popular in Eastern Europe.

········ EARLY UNIFORM BUTTONS ········

To understand why uniform buttons were needed, collectors must first consider the history of uniforms, which are not chosen by the wearer but by an authority in commanding the wearer. Some historians claim that uniforms, by this definition, go back to the pre-Christian era in Greece, Rome, Egypt, or Persia.

Two of the oldest uniform designs still in use are those of the Swiss Guard at the Vatican which dates to 1506 and of the Tower Warders at the Tower of London which also dates to the sixteenth century. However, neither design emphasizes the buttons. Buttons with an organization's unique design first appeared during the 1600s, and an ancestor of the British Firmin Company was listed as a button maker as early as 1677.

In Europe among the first non-military units to receive uniforms were the postal services and customs/border guard personnel. In the Danish Postal Museum in Copenhagen, there is a fine collection of uniforms dating back several centuries, each with buttons bearing the traditional postal horn and the cypher of the monarch. Throughout continental Europe, the earliest railroads were government operations, so employees wore the current button design made for the local principality or kingdom. In fact, this practice continued in Germany on the Prussian State Railway (KPEB) until World War I.

Livery buttons, worn by the household and stable staffs of noble families primarily in England and Europe, are uniform buttons by definition, although the National Button Society classifies them as ordinary clothing buttons. They gave the wearer certain privileges, particularly in towns near the seat of the noble family. Each button usually bore the family crest or some part of the coat-of-arms. Many of these handsome, and greatly sought-after, buttons are found today. Most are stamped from one piece of brass and plated, but some are made from black horn or hard rubber, versions worn while the family and its servants were in mourning. It is not known when the first livery buttons were made, but some designs and buttons date back to the 1700s.

The earliest British railway companies had special buttons made for wear by their employees, and the same trend occurred with buttons for European shipping and ferry companies' uniforms.

······· NORTH AMERICAN TRENDS ·······

However, American and Canadian companies were not swift to follow before 1860, but by the 1860s and 1870s many major American railroads issued unique button designs to their uniformed employees. Some horse car lines, particularly in Philadelphia and Boston, put their employees in uniforms with distinctive buttons in the 1860s, but it was not until the late 1880s when both cable cars and electric trolleys appeared that the practice became common in North America. After all, the public wanted to know that this character who came through the cars demanding money was an employee of the company. Many companies supplied well-cut, high-quality uniforms costing perhaps half a month's wages to all employees who came in contact with the public, and these uniforms were replaced periodically at little or no cost to the employee.

The four decades prior to World War I saw a proliferation of button designs made for fraternal and veterans organizations and for commercial and municipal operations. Uniforms were used to identify personnel who had the right to enter a private home to collect the money from early gas meters and pay-telephone coin boxes, or to read electric meters. Buttons worn by these employees often showed gas meters, electric light bulbs, or telephone parts in their designs. Uniforms were also used to create an attractive appearance by employees who could not afford to dress well on their meager pay; elevator operators in department stores, bellhops and doormen in hotels, and milkmen all had buttons incorporating the company's logo.

Less common are buttons from uniforms of ambulance drivers and attendants – the design often showed a walking man with a doctor's bag in hand – or employees of various World's Fairs in the US and Canada. Stock designs with various job classifications meant that tailors could apply the appropriate buttons to a uniform; collectors can look for OPERATOR, AGENT, CONDUCTOR, and GRIPMAN, for example. Military prep schools also gave rise to a great number of different designs of "School and University" buttons. The creation of new uniform button designs has been at a low rate over the past 60 years.

Buttons on this page and opposite are all brass unless otherwise indicated; 1 in/ 2.5 cm; European and Canadian uniforms.

1. Spain, Municipal guard.
2. Spain, Infantry.
3. France, Gendarmes (police).
4. Canada, Royal Canadian Air Force, pre-1952.
5. Canada, Royal Canadian Navy, post-1952.
6. Germany, Navy, pre-World War II.
7. Great Britain, Merchant Marines.
8. Great Britain, Navy, pre-1952, horn.
9. Great Britain, Navy, post-1952.
10. Great Britain, Royal Artillery, pre-1952.
11. Great Britain, Royal Air Force, pre-1952.
12. Great Britain, Royal Air Force, post-1952.
13. Great Britain, Police, pre-1952.
14. Great Britain, Army Regiment, Highland Light Infantry, post-1962.
15. Great Britain, General List (army); plastic, World War II.
16. Great Britain, Auxiliary Fire Service, World War II.
17. Great Britain, Police (Somerset).
18. Great Britain, Royal Navy, summer tropical uniform; plastic, pre-1952.
19. Great Britain, Edinburgh University.
20. Great Britain, Queen's College.

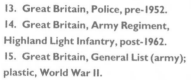

···ALL ABOUT UNIFORM BUTTONS···

New collectors wonder why so many buttons in the same design are in different colors and sizes, or why there are so many different designs for a given organization.

The colors are often an indication of rank. *Gold* (called *yellow* by advanced collectors) is issued to higher ranks – train conductors in North America, for example, or station masters and other management-level employees in Britain, and *silver* (called *white*) to lower ranks like brakemen, porters, motormen, etc.

In addition, in Britain and France, it is common to issue different designs for different pay levels or departments of an organization.

Size is an indication of where a button was to be worn. The normal size is just under 1in/2.5cm in diameter and is usually worn on a jacket or blouse. Larger buttons were used primarily on overcoats or great coats; it was easier to handle a larger button with cold or wet hands. Smaller sizes were used on caps, jacket, or cuffs, at the ends of gold braid, or as decorations on the swallowtail of the splendid coats once favored by some American conductors.

In the nineteenth century, the rank of the wearer could be determined in most European countries by the amount of gold braid (called *gold lace* by military collectors), the number of buttons on the uniform, and the size and shape of the hat. Tricorns and feathered "fore and aft" hats were commonly worn on German railroads by lower, middle, and upper managers.

"Fox Patent," threaded rim, screw-post reversible, and other patented designs became popular in the 1880s. These semi-permanent buttons permitted a wearer to convert his dark suit to a uniform by slipping the Fox Patent shell over his suit buttons, or by threading the brass cover of the threaded-rim design over a male-threaded dark suit button. The screw-post reversible had a metal shell with the stamped uniform design on one side and a plain hard rubber face on the other. Unthreading the button and reversing it on the threaded shank could convert the Grand Army of the Republic (GAR) lodge meeting uniform or railroad conductor's jacket into a properly somber Sunday-go-to-meeting suit coat.

This page and opposite: uniform buttons of transportation lines.

Nos 1.–5. Brass US railroad buttons, marked with the logo of the railroad; private railroads no longer exist in the US.
1. Pennsylvania Railroad.
2. Great Northern Railroad.
3. Santa Fe (earlier Atcheson, Topeka, and Santa Fe).
4. Southern Railroad.
5. Illinois Central Railroad.

Nos 6.–10. Land transportation other than railroads.
6. California Street Cable Railroad.
7. Chicago Transit Authority.
8. Boston Elevated Railway.
9. Greyhound Lines.
10. Former United States Trucking Corporation.

Nos 11.–15. Water Transportation flying the US flag.
11. Dollar Line; round-the-world service.
12. Munson Steamship Company.
13. Hoboken Ferry Company.
14. Eastern Steamship Company.
15. Cleveland and Buffalo Line.

Nos 16.–20. Miscellaneous uniform buttons often worn by doormen and elevator operators working in a company's building.
16. Cardy Hotels.
17. Edison Electric Illuminating Company.
18. John Wanamaker Company.
19. Bankers Trust Company.
20. Empire State Building.

Nos 21.–25. Miscellaneous uniform buttons, use for easy identification of employees working away from the company's building or office.
21. Police; Port Chester, New York.
22. US Postal Service.
23. Carnegie Steel Company.
24. Trans World Airlines.
25. Delta Airlines.

··COLLECTING UNIFORM BUTTONS··

Collecting uniform buttons can be expensive, but most uniform buttons are sold by button dealers for less than $10. Uniform buttons authenticated as prior to 1800 are usually from $10 to $250, or more. Wood or bone-baked uniform buttons are equally pricey; cost depends mainly on the number of known examples of a given design.

Livery buttons are plentiful and generally less than $10, depending on the design and the condition of the button. Those classed as "ladies" designs which display a diamond-shaped lozenge, and "mourning" issues in black horn or dark painted metal are more expensive. Those with two or three crests on the same button are also very desirable and, therefore, more expensive.

Uniform buttons from military units, either companies or massive armies of World War I and II, vary in price by the country of origin, age of the unit or of the design, the size of

the unit and the number of buttons issued, and the romance associated with the specific unit. The common American General Service design with an eagle is often collected for the manufacturer's backmark, as are the "walking postman over POD" United States Post Office Department buttons.

Someone with a knowledge of the official designs of crowns adopted by the countries of the world can quickly assemble a fine collection of foreign military and governmental buttons from dealers' stocks with little cash outlay.

There are books on specific areas, such as transportation, to help the novice collector, but specialization in areas for which there are no books requires research to check validity. The beginning collector should try to work with a more experienced collector to detect fakes and reproductions. By handling both old and modern versions of the same button, a collector can develop the skill needed to prevent paying antique prices for today's production.

No. 2121

CHAPTER 10

Other Button Collectibles

Many button collectors also include items related to buttons, such as buckles, cuff buttons (or studs as they are sometimes called), buttonhooks, shoe button covers, and bridle rosettes, in their collections. Many of the cuff buttons and buckles found today are made of the same materials and have the same designs as buttons, because they were popular during the Victorian era. Buttonhooks were also used during the same period. Shoe button covers emerged as a fashion item in the 1920s. Bridle rosettes had their heyday from the mid-nineteenth century and disappeared around the end of use of the horse-drawn vehicle in 1918.

CUFF BUTTONS

Cuff buttons consist of a button-like disk coupled to a smaller disk or a patented fastener. The fastener always has a post-like portion, thus giving the name "stud" to the whole fastener.

Studs were made for several purposes: for fastening cuffs, men's vests, ladies' shirtwaists, and as decorative inserts for the lapel. The studs for cuffs and vests were similar to jewelry in construction and often in decoration as well. The studs made for ladies' shirtwaists between 1890 and 1920 were porcelain decorated with hand painting or decals of design such as flowers or female heads. Lapel studs were anything from souvenir items (for example, commemorating the 1876 Centennial celebration in Philadelphia), to political campaigns buttons, to membership "emblems" in a lodge or fraternal organization.

The earliest studs were plain one-piece buttons, made of bone or metal. They were difficult to maneuver in a stiff collar or cuff. Then came separable buttons, the two parts firmly joined by an easily unfastened spring catch, which were thought to be the perfect solution.

Shortly before 1880, an enterprising Frenchman invented a button with a hinged shoe that could be turned edgewise, inserted into the cuff, and then tipped back to its original position. It was still rather clumsy, but was the forerunner of the "lever" button.

The Acme lever button was patented by WW Covell of Fred J Marcy & Co., a button manufacturer in Providence, Rhode

Island. Lever buttons at once became favorites of the public, and soon a host of other manufacturers began to make them. With increased competition came a reduction in price and consequently in profit. The leading makers then strove to outdistance their rivals by superiority and variety of design on the front of the button. Thus, we see studs in all of the materials and techniques used in making buttons. In Marcy's packing room alone, 6,000 different designs could be found.

Studs can be collected in pairs, but many collectible examples are found only as single buttons. They are more difficult to mount than buttons, but they are beautiful small art. Although they are not found as frequently as buttons, in many cases buttons with the same design or construction are more expensive.

ABOVE

Cuff buttons or studs were used by gentlemen from the early nineteenth century into the twentieth century to fasten cuffs and shirt fronts and to change the style, without changing the design, of the shirt.

1 2 3 4 5 6 7 8

BUCKLES

Buckles are probably as old as buttons and have long served a similar purpose. Early bronze buckles for clasping thick belts and fastening girdles and mantles were important articles of dress. In China, buckles and belt hooks of gilded metal, jade, and ivory were made for royalty, dignitaries, and officials. Throughout the Middle Ages, buckles were in common use as dress and mantle fastenings, and a variety of materials was used. By the late fourteenth century, shoes were buckled at the instep and garters were often fastened by ornamental buckles. During the eighteenth and nineteenth centuries, European craftsmen were designing elaborate buckles using mostly the same materials as buttons and decorated similarly.

Buckles were the height of fashion in the late nineteenth and early twentieth centuries. The buckles commonly found today from that era fall into two categories: two-piece with a shank or shanks and clasp findings, probably used as cloak fasteners, and one-piece with or without chapes used as belt and sash fasteners.

ABOVE

Like the buttons they often imitated, the gentleman's cuff buttons or studs used a variety of materials, providing a kind of jewelry for the middle-class man.

1. Glass with overlay trim in circular pattern and border design.
2. Fan-shaped brass button with pearl applied and decorated with cut steels.
3. Mosaic design of birds and flowers on a black glass base and mounted on low-grade gold.
4. Chinese dog of carved stone.
5. Silver inlayed in tortoise-shell of eagle for the 1876 US centennial.
6. Silver salamander; size indicates it was probably a shirt stud.
7. Painted porcelain stud intended for a shirt front.
8. Scene under glass mounted in gilded brass.

LEFT
LEFT

Painted porcelain studs became popular for shirtwaists in women's fashion from the 1880s on, and women often learned to paint their own studs as they painted china plates in the early twentieth century.

1.,2.,3.,4. Painted studs with fixed shanks. 5.,6.,7. Probably transfer designs which were then enhanced with hand painting, just as ceramic buttons were made; fixed shank.

ABOVE

Elaborate buckles, decorated with a variety of techniques incorporating all materials, complemented women's costumes by drawing attention to the accentuated waists.

1. Brass decorated with red glass to suggest gemstones; c 1890; probably for evening wear.
2. Celluloid to simulate snake skin; probably for daywear.
3. Carved gray pearl of love birds, decorated with cut steels.

Button-type buckles with clasps can be found in many materials, but metal is most common. These buckles seem to have been made in the same way and from the same designs as metal pictorial buttons. Many of these buckles have been converted to buttons by removing the clasp findings. Buttons that were buckles can be identified by the bit of solder left on the edge when the buckle clasp was removed.

Belt and sash buckles were made by the thousand. Far more exquisite than the cloak buckles, they were made in every conceivable shape in many materials, including cut steel, enamel, glass, paste, and pearl. Many, such as those with Art Nouveau designs, were highly embellished with embossing and chasing. When Bakelite and celluloid, the precursors to plastic, appeared, they were used for making buckles as well as buttons.

ABOVE

Buckles or cloak closures were manufactured to match buttons on the jacket or the coat of the woman of the late 1880s, when picture buttons were very popular.

1. Cloak closure with matching button of Mme Butterfly with cut steel fan.
2. Wood background on buckle which may have been used as decoration on the collar as well as at the waist, with matching buttons; called camel ride or desert rider.

LEFT

In the late nineteenth century, belts were often made of fabric which matched the dress and the buckle, like this cut steel butterfly design, which provided contrasting decoration at the woman's waist.

Later in the twentieth century, these elaborate buckles were superseded by cheap mass-produced plastic and white metal examples. Although plentiful, they are valued by true collectors because of their lack of artistry and craftsmanship.

Many fine collectible buckles from the late nineteenth and early twentieth century can be found today, and collectors can look for matching sets of buttons and buckles.

················· B U T T O N H O O K S ·················

Buttonhooks were used from the mid-nineteenth to the early twentieth century to get buttons through buttonholes. Then, buttons were commonly used on shoes and gloves, which were difficult to maneuver without help. At first household articles were used to get the buttons through stiff new leather or to button long gloves. Wooden gadgets tended to break, but articles of metal, bone, and ivory held up. American ingenuity came to the rescue and invented the buttonhook. Buttonhooks range in size from approximately 5in/12.5cm for a glove buttoner to 9in/23cm for a shoe buttoner. Buttonhooks that slid out of pocket knives or out of their own closed container were also made. Although these are usually made of plain metal and not very attractive, their uniqueness makes them real finds for the collector.

Buttonhooks can be found in different materials. Hardwoods turned on a lathe were used for handles, but they tended to crack. Metal handles were made in two parts, then soldered together. Some metal handles were made in the shape of a ring, which meant the hook could be hung up. The most interesting of these ring-handled buttonhooks are those with names stamped on them, including names of stores, individuals, cities, or, rarely, states.

Some of the most beautiful buttonhooks were made of silver. Buttonhooks marked *Sterling* can be found and on some a trademark or the name of the company is seen. The patterns used for knives or silverware were also used for buttonhooks. If the handle shines, but has no markings, it is probably a silver wash, now known as silverplate.

Initially ivory was used, but when it became scarce in about 1870, a new material called pyrolin was used to manufacture buttonhooks. Many were made to imitate ivory

BELOW
Buttonhooks made the fastening of small buttons used on high-topped shoes and kid gloves of the late nineteenth and the early twentieth century less of a chore, and their decoration made the hooks look less utilitarian and more beautiful.

1. Hook in its original box. The satin lining indicates it was a prized possession.
2.,3. Molded metal handles decorate this hook.
4.,5. Hooks often carried manufacturers' information or logos from advertisers.
6. Ivory, as well as other precious materials, were used in the handles of button hooks for the wealthy.

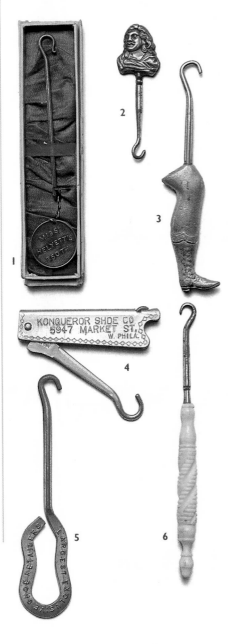

ABOVE

In the 1920s and 1930s, the buttons used to fasten the straps on Mary Jane shoes were covered with decorated shoe button covers.

2.,4.,6. These show the backs of the shoe button covers indicating how they slid over the plain button.

1.,3.,5. Metal stamped covers with paint applied to highlight the designs. These were manufactured cheaply and quickly; often buckles matched the covers.

7. Black glass was used, especially for evening wear; the shield design with light silver luster fit the Art Deco design.

8. Modern plastic encasing glitter showed the most up-to-date use of modern materials.

ABOVE

Bridle rosettes were used as fasteners on harnesses; plain metal designs like the heart were popular in the mid nineteenth century. Highly decorated bridle rosettes became popular at the end of the nineteenth century.

and amber, and a collector must look carefully not to be fooled. Plastic handles from this period were made in all colors of the rainbow and were often part of matching dresser sets.

Many varieties of buttonhooks can still be found. The most common and inexpensive are metal and plastic. A real find is a buttonhook still in its original box.

⋯⋯⋯⋯⋯ SHOE BUTTON COVERS ⋯⋯⋯⋯⋯

Shoe button covers were used in the early part of the twentieth century, when shoes had a strap that crossed the instep and fastened with a button on one side. The covers were used to dress up shoes with plain, pin-shanked buttons for evening wear. The typical back has a fastening arrangement that slipped over the shoe button. Other, more complex fasteners can also be found.

Commonly found materials include cut steel, white or gilded metal with or without paint, and metal with glass pastes. Enamel and molded glass with foil inclusions are rarer.

Shoe button covers can be collected singly or in pairs. They can often be found by picking through old jewelry. Many people do not know what these small objects are, so they may be a bargain.

⋯⋯⋯⋯⋯ BRIDLE ROSETTES ⋯⋯⋯⋯⋯

Bridle rosettes, used for decorating bridles, have large, rectangular bar shanks through which the leather bridle strap could be slipped. They probably appeared in the mid-nineteenth century and disappeared with horse-drawn vehicles, in about 1918.

One type found commonly today is the bright paper cutout mounted under a heavy glass front, which is either domed or flat, and set in a metal back. Metal rosettes are also common. Rosettes were also made in hard rubber and composition, but they did not wear well and so are less often found. Designs range from conventional and horse-related items to dogs and flowers. Rosettes made in right and left pairs are rare.

············· BIBLIOGRAPHY ·············

Albert, Lillian Smith and Jane Ford Adams *The Button Sampler* (Gramercy Publishing Company, New York, 1951).
Albert, Lillian Smith and Kathryn Kent *The Complete Button Book* (Doubleday and Company, Garden City, NY, 1949).
Betensley, Bertha L, *Buttonhooks to Trade – to Treasure* (Chicago, 1958).
Coysh, A W *British Art Pottery 1870–1940* (Charles E. Tuttle Company, Rutland, Vermont, 1976).
Epstein, Diana *Buttons* (Walker and Company, New York, 1968).
Epstein, Diana and Millicent Safro *Buttons* (Harry N. Abrams Inc., New York, 1991).
Ford, Grace Horney *The Button Collector's History* (Springfield, MA, 1943).
Houart, Victor *Buttons: A Collector's Guide* (Charles Scribner & Sons, New York, 1977).
Hughes, Elizabeth and Marion Lester *The Big Book of Buttons* (2nd ed. New Leaf Publishers, Sedgwick, ME, 1991).
Jones, W. Unite *The Button Industry in this Country* (Sir Isaac Pitman and Sons, London, 1924. Reprinted with permission by Edith Fuoss, 1946).
Luscomb, Sally C *The Collector's Encyclopedia of Buttons* (Crown
McNulty, Lyndi Stewart *Price Guide to Plastic Collectibles* (Wallace-Homestead, Greensboro, NC, 1987).
National Button Society *A Complete Classification of Clear and Colored Glass Buttons* (Revised ed 1986).
National Button Society *Guidelines for Collecting China Buttons* 1970 (Available from the Society).
Schiff, Stefan O *Buttons: Art in Miniature* (Lancaster Miller Publishers, Berkeley, CA, 1979).
Whittemore, Joyce *The Book of Buttons* (Dorling Kindersley, Inc., New York, 1992).

UNIFORMS AND UNIFORM BUTTONS
Albert, Alphaeus H *Record of American Uniform and Historical Buttons* (Hightstown, NJ, 1969. Third ed. 1976).
Froggatt, David J *Railway Buttons, Badges, and Uniforms* (Ian Allen Ltd., London, 1986).

Henneking, Gunther, and Wolfgang Koch *Die Uniform Des Deutschen Eisenbahners* (Eisenbahn-Kurier Verlag GmbH. Frelburg im Brelsgau, Germany, 1980).
Johnson, David F *Uniform Buttons, American Armed Forces 1784–1948* (Two volumes. Century House, Watkins Glen, NY, 1948).
McGuinn, William F and Bruce S Bazelon *American Military Button Makers and Dealers: Their Backmarks and Dates* (McLean, VA, 1984).
Parkyn, Major H G, O.B.E. *Shoulder-Belt Plates and Buttons* (Gale and Polden, Ltd., Wellington Press, Aldershot, England, 1956).
Ripley, Howard *Buttons of the British Army 1855–1970* (Arms and Armour Press, Levanthal Ltd., London, revised 1973).
Police Forces of Great Britain and Ireland: Their Amalgamations and their Buttons (R Hazell and Company, Lavenham Press, Lavenham, England, 1983).
Squires, Gwen *Buttons, A Guide for Collectors* (Frederick Muller Ltd., London, 1972).
Thompson, Major Roy J C *Camp Badges and Insignia of the Canadian Army* Vol. 3: 1953–1973 (Nova Scotia, Canada, 1973).
Van Court, Donald P TRANSPORTATION UNIFORM SERIES
    Volume I – Railroad (Madison, NJ, 1987).
    Volume II – Transit (Madison, NJ, 1991).
Vicker-Smith, Lt. Evelyn, R.O.C. *Uniform Buttons* (Enfield Arsenal Manual-Mark 1, Kitchener House Publisher, Washington, D.C., 1965).

PERIODICALS
Just Buttons: "Twentieth Century Realistics," November, 1967; "Dorset Buttons," January, 1969; "Death's Head Buttons," February, 1969; "Wooden Buttons," August, 1976; "Buttons of Pearl and Shell," August, 1977; "Satsuma," September, 1977.
National Button Society Bulletin: "The Story of Lucite," January, 1984; "Button making as a Pauper Trade," September, 1954; "Proposed Classification of Celluloid Buttons," May/June, 1970; "Cleaning Buttons," December, 1986; "Motiwala: The Indian Master of Modern Buttons," October, 1990.

········ USEFUL ADDRESSES ·········

England
British Button Society
c/o Monica Jones
27 Pitch & Pay Park
Sneyd Park, Bristol BS9 1NL

Sheila Bird
(collector and dealer)
The Cottage, Nottingham
Weymouth, Dorset DT3 4BJ

Rita Stephenson
(collector and dealer)
151 Portobello Road, London

Jessie's Button Box
Great Western Antique Centre
Bartlett Street, Bath

Dorothy Speculo
(collector and dealer)
17 High Beeches
Gerrards Cross
Bucks SL9 7HX

Bristol Button Club
c/o P. Wake, TOR View Cottage
Galhampton Hill, Yeovil
Somerset BA22 7AE

United States
National Button Society
c/o Miss Lois Pool
2733 Juno Place
Akron, Ohio 44333–4137

Tender Buttons
143 E. 43rd Street, New York
NY 10021

M.W. Speights
(collector and dealer)
5707 Greencraig, Houston
TX 77035

W. Tice and Company
(collector/dealer of uniform
buttons), P.O. Box 8491, Essex
VT 05451

Donald Van Court
(collector/dealer of uniform
buttons), 41 Hillcrest Road
Madison NJ 07940–2559

Lucille Weingarten
(collector and dealer)
1183 Lime Drive
Sunnyvale, CA 94087

Jane Beck (collector and dealer)
271 Green Bay Road
Cedarburg, WI 53012

Renaissance Buttons
826 W. Armitage, Chicago
IL 60614

········ ACKNOWLEDGEMENTS ·······

Special appreciation is extended to Donald Van Court for writing "Uniform Buttons, Chapter 9" and to Virginia Esten for contributing to the chapter. They provided the buttons to illustrate the content. Without them we would not have been able to present a complete collector's guide. Also, thanks is extended to those experts in the field of button collecting who have published their research on which this book is based. Elizabeth Hughes, Diana Epstein, Millicent Safro, Lillian Smith Albert, M W Speights, Stefan Schiff, Sally Luscomb, Jane Ford Adams, and Grace Horney have preserved information which is valuable to every collector, no matter how experienced. Our debt to them is beyond payment.

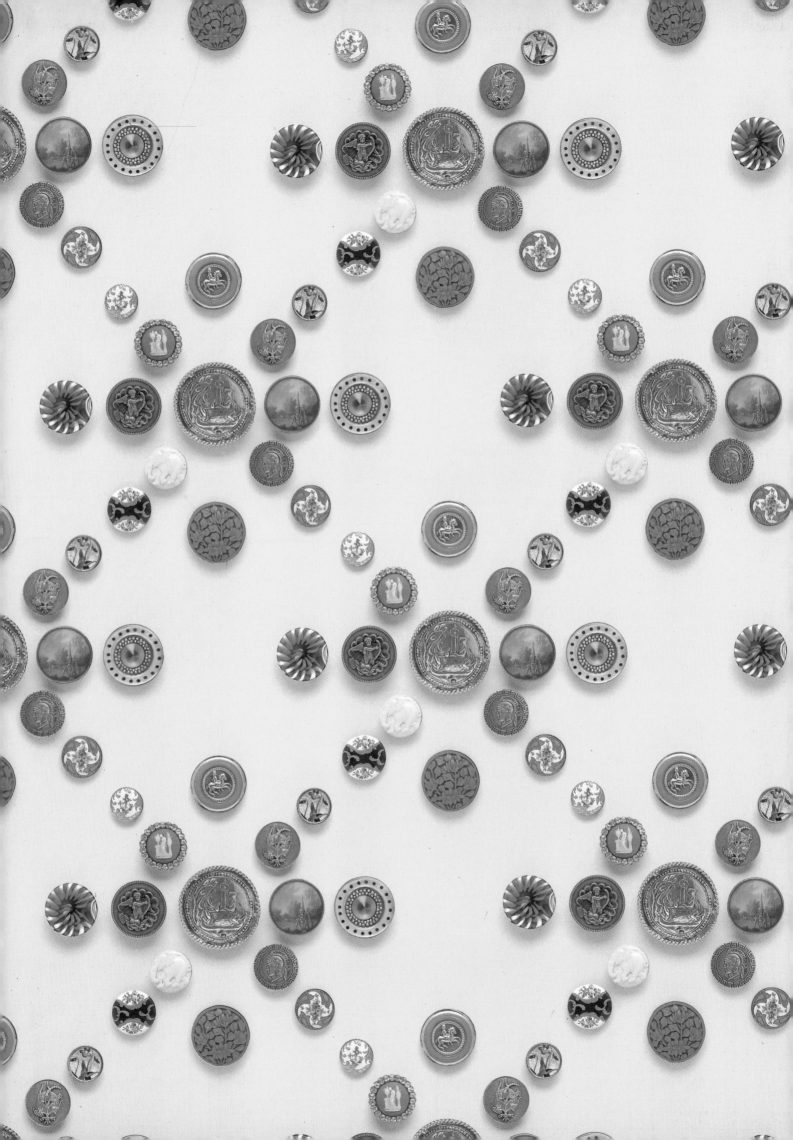